# SOUP

## for Every Body

**ALSO BY JOANNA PRUESS**

Supermarket Confidential
Eat Tea (with John Harney)

# SOUP
## for Every Body

LOW CARB, HIGH PROTEIN, VEGETARIAN, AND MORE

by JOANNA PRUESS

With a foreword and nutritional information by
Lauren R. Braun, RD, LD

THE LYONS PRESS
GUILFORD, CONNECTICUT
AN IMPRINT OF THE GLOBE PEQUOT PRESS

The Lyons Press is an imprint of The Globe Pequot Press.

10  9  8  7  6  5  4  3  2  1

Photographs on pages 47, 55, 57, 63, 89, 95, 103, and 122 © Photo Disc; photographs on pages 58, 87, and 152 © photos.com. All other photographs © Liesa Cole Photography.

Printed in China

Designed by LeAnna Weller Smith

ISBN 1-59228-565-1

Library of Congress Cataloging-in-Publication Data is available on file.

To Nicole, Ben and Justin:
As always, you are my muses and inspiration.
Thanks for many years of sharing bowls of soup.


To Bob Lape, who stirred the pot and my heart,
for his support and love.

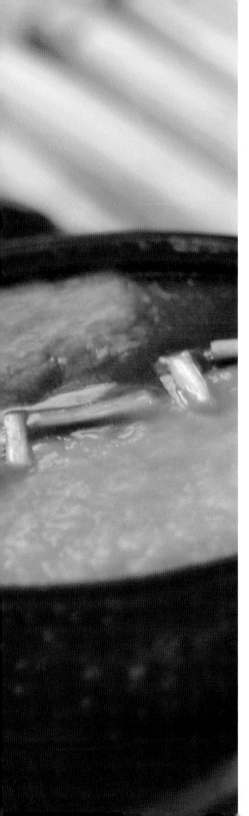

# Contents

# Acknowledgments

I could not have chosen a better time than this past winter to write a book about soup. With far more than the average amounts of snow on the ground, and glacial winds often howling outside, I never minded the ever-present pots of soups simmering on my stove. They perfumed my house and brought new and old friends to my kitchen.

These months also permitted me to recall many happy memories about soups shared with friends and family over the years. Thank you Jay Cassell for coming over for a bowl of corn and shrimp chowder and then letting me gather my favorite soup recipes and memories into a book.

While the weather kept *me* indoors, I'm indebted to many intrepid friends and colleagues who willingly braved the elements to come by and check on my progress. Their suggestions and encouragement were invaluable.

Some of my most loyal supporters included Rick and Charlie Waln; Marcie Sweigert, Darien and John Zoppo; Mimi Nelson, Judy Weinstock, Charlie and Eva Gerard; Janet Jussel; Erica Loutsch and my dear neighbor, Marie Lieto. There were also the loyal members of the Soup Club, especially Bebe and Norman Isaacs, Linda Gallagher, and Judy Donovan who eagerly asked what soup I was cooking, week after week.

My friends Sally and Gene Kofke were, as always, a wonderfully receptive audience and discriminating samplers.

Additionally, I'm grateful to Pamela Harding for her thoughtful suggestions for beverages to drink with soups and her astute suggestions for the manuscript.

Lauren Braun, your wisdom and insight gave this book the factual information and credibility it needed to help everyone more fully enjoy soups. Thanks for laughing while still plodding forward.

The group at Liesa Cole Photography brought my soups to life and Leanna Weller Smith's design perfected my vision.

Finally, I am grateful to Ann Treistman, my extraordinary editor at Lyons Press for her wisdom, enthusiasm, attention to detail, and patience with my many questions. You and your team, particularly Larry Dorfman and copyeditor Jane Crosen, did so much to make this book more than a collection of soup recipes.

# Introduction

Some of my first food memories center around bowls of colorful vegetable soup for lunch with my four siblings or cups of clear chicken broth and soda crackers brought to my bed when I was feeling less than one hundred percent. Did I care that they came from a can? Hardly! I probably didn't know the difference. However, I was aware from a very early age that soup always had a positive effect on me.

Over time, with experience and travel, my palate became more sophisticated. I tasted many soups around the world and was seldom disappointed. Every cuisine has its own unique soups—the possible combinations seem endless—but universally they somehow magically afford sustenance and satisfaction to many.

Along the way, I discovered that soups are good for every *body,* as well as everyone. Whether you're lean or hoping to lose some extra pounds, a child or in your ninth decade, a vegetarian or meat lover, rich or poor, there's ample room in your diet for soups. Many recipes are easily modified to conform to today's most popular diets.

Soups also fit today's lifestyle. From age-old classics like split pea soup to contemporary creations, soups are finding favor in today's world because, first and foremost, they make us feel so good. They're the quintessential comfort foods we're all seeking.

We eat soup for lunch, late at night, for dinner and even, by some, for breakfast. One of my favorite meals is a cup of soup and a salad at almost any hour of the day. And that's just one of many good things about soups: their versatility.

In a world where fewer people seem to find time for the pleasures of cooking, not many foods are as simple to make or as versatile. With a couple of chops of a knife or pulses in a food processor, a little of this and of that—be it vegetables, herbs, chicken or leftovers, along with some liquid—becomes a whole meal. And it's very rewarding.

Add a little stock and some fresh herbs to savory leftover stew and it becomes a hearty soup that's far more appealing than reheated fare. For guacamole lovers, when that avocado (even if it's a little past its prime), tomatoes, onions and chile are smoothed with a touch of stock and sour cream, you'll discover a tasty new way to begin a summer meal.

You needn't search far for the ingredients. Compared with how we shopped and cooked even a decade or two ago, today's convenience foods are a boon to soup making. Curried Turkey-Spinach Soup takes minutes to make with purchased turkey cutlets, baby spinach leaves, and curry paste. It's pleasantly sophisticated and almost carbohydrate free. Corn & Shrimp Chowder, similarly made with supermarket fixings, has legions of fans.

For families and crowds, soups like minestrone, gumbo, and chowder are a natural not only because they're so kind to the pocketbook. They're easy to make in big batches and a great way to socially break the ice. With such relaxed fare, conversation easily flows. Soups freeze well, can be made ahead of time, and get better with reheating after storage in the refrigerator.

And, according to some sources, certain soups have restorative properties—especially chicken broth, legendary as a cure for the common cold and flu. Today doctors acknowledge that those delectable vapors wafting up your nose from the bowl can really help relieve congestion. On page 102, you'll find the perfect chicken soup. Another soup to cure what ails you is Ginger Lentil Soup.

Novice and accomplished cooks alike find soup making easy. It's also unique in the culinary repertoire. Few foods can claim to be elegant and rustic, hearty and delicate, delicious when served hot and cold as a first course or whole meal and even dessert. Winter or summer, any season of the year is soup time. And, happily there are very few "no's" in the process.

Some of this book's recipes, like Split Pea with and without meat, Clam Chowder Providence-Style, and Hearty Roasted Onion Soup with Parmesan Crostini, are my interpretations of classics. In others, like Roasted Sweet Potato & Onions Soup scented with Bourbon, Broccoli-Almond Soup and Roasted Red Pepper Soup with Mole Sauce, I borrowed age-old cooking techniques and flavors from around the world to create contemporary recipes. Still others are favorites contributed by friends.

In recent years, I've been called the Soup Lady around my town because there's always a pot or two simmering on my stove or containers in my refrigerator and freezer. I even launched a Soup Club where those in the know stop by to buy pints and quarts of my homemade creations. The feedback has been terrific.

What follows is not a treatise on soup. It's a collection of favorite soups and amusing anecdotes I've gathered over the years. Most of these soups are incredibly simple to prepare. I hope many of them will meet your expectations for delicious and satisfying meals.

To make good soups you simply need to love them. And I do.


Joanna Pruess
Bedford Hills, New York
February 2004

# How This Book Can Help You

### Nutritional Information

Everyone in America seems to have dietary concerns, and there's an enormous industry trying to promote ways to help us get healthier and look better. Recently, many people have jumped on the low-carbohydrate diet bandwagon to lose weight. A look at supermarkets, restaurants, and even drugstores reveal the dramatic proliferation of low-carb foods.

As counterintuitive as they may seem, the South Beach, Atkins, and Zone diets that include ample amounts of meat and fish as well as fats seem to melt away pounds and inches, especially in the midsection area, for many people. They're also said to lower "bad" or LDL cholesterol levels and raise "good" or HDL cholesterol. I applaud these dieters' efforts and have included many carb-smart recipes to support their endeavors.

Other dietary concerns relating to health and/or lifestyle choices include reducing saturated fats or eliminating animal products from one's diet. Some people count calories to control their weight, while an increasing number of people discover they are lactose intolerant and omit dairy products.

When reading recipes, I think it's helpful to see at a glance how the dishes—in this case soups—fit into your personal regimen and lifestyle. You'll find these indicators near the recipe title to show how each soup "measures up" dietarily. The complete nutritional analysis appears at the end of each recipe.

As useful as these details are, this book is primarily about appealing, delicious soups. Because we are often tempted by how a dish looks before we even taste it, many recipes include a final garnish to make them more attractive or to hint at the predominant ingredients in the soup.

It can be as simple as a sprinkle of minced herbs. In Broccoli-Almond Soup, a tiny broccoli floret immediately identifies the potentially mysterious green vegetable. Some garnishes may be relatively high in calories or fat, like pesto, but they're also low carb. Additions like crostini really enhance the soup. Although they aren't especially diet friendly, I think they are worth the indulgence. Unless otherwise indicated by the word "optional" in parenthesis, the nutritional breakdown includes the recommended topping.

You can use the toppings, omit them, use a small amount, or substitute other garnishes more appropriate to your diet. Garnishes and suggested additions also have nutritional details so you can calculate the total for every soup.

For the nutritional information, including suggested healthful additions and ways to modify certain recipes to suit your needs, I turned to Lauren Braun, a registered and licensed dietician. In 1989, Lauren founded Nutritional Lifestyle Designs (www.nutrismart.com). Since then, she has successfully guided numerous individuals and families to healthy, satisfying resolutions for many difficult-to-pinpoint food-related conditions, including weight control, heart disease, diabetes, gastrointestinal disorders, and specific food intolerances. For the past 15 years, Lauren has analyzed the recipes in my "Prepared Food Focus" columns for the National Association for the Specialty Food Trade magazine.

The following indicators (explained in detail on pages 11–15) will help you decide which soups, garnishes, and ingredients fit your dietary needs. In some cases, these indicators relate to an option that you can take (i.e., using soy yogurt to make a recipe vegan) while in others, they reflect the nutritional content of the soup as described. This will be clear within each recipe. Look for:

LOW CARB

HIGH PROTEIN

SMART FAT

LOW CALORIE

VEGETARIAN OR VEGAN

## Portions

Throughout the book, I give the suggested number of portions each recipe makes. Typically it's 1 cup as a first course and slightly less for dessert. Russian Cabbage & Beef Borscht is a generous one-dish main course. You may want to serve 1½ cups, or even more, for hungry eaters. Mighty Minestrone can be served either in large bowls as an entrée or in a cup as an appetizer.

Therefore, the suggested number of servings equals the number of 8-ounce cups in each recipe. Since we all have different-size appetites, and many people like second helpings, this will help you to determine if you want to double a recipe based on how much soup you can comfortably eat.

## Serving Soup

This brings up another subject—how to serve soup. Nowhere is it written that conventional cups or bowls (or even matched sets) or traditional tureens must be used. A tiny cup of light soup might serve as an interlude between courses. If you have espresso demitasse cups, press

them into service. On the other hand, a hollowed-out pumpkin makes a dramatic soup tureen for Pumpkin–Black Bean Soup. For charming and edible soup bowls, hollow out individual round rolls made with firm-textured bread. This is discussed in the chapter on Garnishes, Condiments & Other Tasty Additions.

## Stock Options

Auguste Escoffier wrote in *Le Guide Culinaire*, "Stocks are the fundamental basis, the elements of first necessity without which nothing can be accomplished. If he is given insufficient or low-quality ingredients with which to perform, the cook cannot aspire to greatness." These rich, clear, homemade liquids can distinguish good soup from a masterpiece.

Realistically, however, many people don't always have homemade stock awaiting them on top of the stove, let alone in the refrigerator or freezer (even though it's easy enough to do). So your next question may be, do I buy stocks? Well, yes, particularly if I am making rustic soups where the stock is more of a thinner than a major contribution to the soup's final taste. But I'm careful what I buy, avoiding stocks that contain preservatives and lots of salt.

For ethereally delicate soups like Sautéed Salsify Soup with White Truffle Oil, where every ingredient can be tasted, I make my own stock. For vegetable stock, an easy habit to adopt is saving the peels and trimmings from onions, celery, carrots, etc. and simmering them together with herbs. At the end of this book there's a whole chapter's worth of recipes for making a savory spectrum of homebrewed stocks.

Increasingly, you can buy some pretty serviceable ready-made stocks in the freezer section of the supermarket, in natural foods stores, and in aseptic boxes. An extremely useful way to buy stocks is in little pucks manufactured by More Than Gourmet (www.morethangourmet.com). When unopened, these small packages are shelf stable and take up almost no space in your pantry. In a pinch, even canned stocks can be refreshed by simmering some fresh herbs and a few vegetables in them for 10–15 minutes (see page 146).

One more word about stock and other liquids in soups: the amounts suggested in each recipe should be viewed as a guideline, because ingredients can vary in their porosity and texture. Therefore you may need additional stock, milk, water, etc. to achieve the optimal consistency.

## Equipment

Making great soups requires few pieces of equipment. My favorites include:
- An electric blender to make velvety-smooth soups, especially when the ratio of liquids to solids is high.
- A food processor to finely chop vegetables like carrots, celery, and onions that are the aromatic base for many soups, and to purée soup ingredients from chunky to smooth, especially where the ratio of solids to liquid is high.

- An immersion blender or wand—a useful tool to put directly into a deep pot to chop cooked soup ingredients without transferring them to a blender or food processor.
- A couple of heavy, deep pots—a 2½-quart pot, a 5- to 6-quart Dutch oven or casserole, and an 8½-quart Dutch oven or stockpot in which to cook soups without risk of spills. Tall pots allow liquids to simmer and concentrate the flavors. Additionally, I use an 8- and 10-inch skillet.
- A couple of ½-cup-capacity ladles, for serving.
- Large and small fine-gauge strainers to strain liquids and, after puréeing ingredients, to achieve perfectly smooth soups.
- A skimmer to remove scum from the surface of simmering soups.
- Cheesecloth or paper towels to line strainers for catching small impurities in liquids, especially the liquor from reconstituted dried mushrooms.
- A good vegetable peeler and, of course, sharp knives.

## Storage

Unless indicated, most soups in this book will keep for about three days in your refrigerator. After that, you should bring the soup back to a boil if you aren't going to eat it right away. Then you can keep it another day or two. Also, most soups can be frozen in airtight containers, such as tightly sealing plastic tubs and heavy, airtight zippered plastic bags. They should keep for three months. As a rule of thumb, soups with meat, poultry, beans, and vegetables freeze well. In my experience, anything involving freezing potatoes (other than commercially frozen french fries or hash browns) turns them to watery mush. And soups containing sour cream or buttermilk are a freezer no-no.

## A Brief Word about Salt

Because each of us has a personal preference for how much salt we like in our foods, most of the recipes in this book say "salt to taste." However, unless you are severely limiting your salt intake, please think about adding at least a half or whole teaspoon of salt to a recipe that serves four. This is not an excessive amount and, as the French say, it gives value to the other ingredients and makes them sparkle. When choosing salt, I prefer sea salt for its purity.

You will notice that there is no nutritional information on sodium—use salt as your diet and taste dictate. Don't forget to include the sodium levels in your broth when calculating this.

# How to Use This Book

By Lauren R. Braun, RD, LD

I've been helping people to create healthy diets for nearly 20 years, and I've found soup an easy way to keep my clients happy and satisfied. Soup feeds a person's senses and body, so that rather than feeling hungry or deprived, we feel good inside and out.

With so many varieties, soups can fit nearly every dietary need. I've worked with Joanna Pruess's recipes for more than 15 years, and I have always been impressed by the variety of soups she creates.

Joanna's soups are delicious and often quite elegant, as well as simple to prepare and tailored to healthy diets. In this unique cookbook, I've provided information on the nutrition of each soup and suggested ways that soups will fit each individual's dietary needs. In all cases, I have used the first option given in each ingredient list to calculate the nutritional values. (For example, when a recipe calls for cream, milk, or soy creamer, I use cream.) As you read this book, the following indicators will help you easily identify or modify the recipes as necessary:

## LOW CARB

Most low-carbohydrate diets restrict the number of carbohydrates allowed in your total caloric intake from a low of 10 percent to a "generous" 30 percent, which in a 1,500-calorie intake would be 112 grams of carbohydrate. Since this is the total allotment for a day, you need to see how many grams of carbohydrates each dish adds and how it fits in with the other kinds of foods you may want to eat. For the purpose of this book, we have defined low-carb recipes as those that provide 20 grams of "net carbs" per serving or less (see next page for definition).

Carbohydrates come in two basic forms: simple and complex. Simple carbohydrates are foods made from white flour and white sugar—such as breads, cakes, and cookies—and are hollow calories because they convert to sugar quickly with very few nutrients.

There are two groups of complex carbohydrates: high fiber and low fiber. High-fiber (high-cellulose) vegetable foods are the healthiest choices for human nutrition. Intake of these foods is associated with lowered incidences of hypertension, cancer, arthritis, and diabetes. Broccoli, cabbage, asparagus, broccoli rabe (rapini), spinach, and leafy greens are good examples of high-fiber foods.

Simple carbs include bananas, tomatoes, most squashes, white breads and pastas, potatoes, and white rice. Whole grains, wild and brown rice, legumes, as well as whole-grain breads and pastas in moderation, provide complex carbohydrates, vitamins, minerals, and fiber. Dietary patterns high in grain products and fiber have been associated with decreased risk of cardiovascular disease.

Soups may be low in carbohydrates, as you will find in many of the recipes in this book. In other soups, there is an option to omit the carbohydrate-rich food. To determine a soup's "net carbs," subtract the grams of fiber from the grams of carbs, making many soups in this book acceptable for low-carb diets. However, it's important to remember that carbohydrates *in moderation* are not necessarily a bad thing when viewed as part of a balanced diet.

Many of the soups in this book allow for a natural balance of blood sugars by being an excellent source of protein and fats. The **glycemic index** measures how fast a food is likely to raise your blood sugar and can be helpful for managing blood sugars. For example, if your blood sugar is low and continuing to drop during exercise, it would be wise to eat a high-fiber carbohydrate with a good source of protein that will raise your blood sugar quickly. Most of the soups in this book will do that for you naturally.

### Tasty Carb-Friendly Additions

Several soups in this book have enticing toppings or condiments that add color, texture, and flair to them without compromising a low-carbohydrate diet. Some of these include purchased basil or homemade Lemon-Parsley Pesto (page 92), tapenade, Rouille (page 97), Aïoli (page 98), and roasted red pepper purée.

### Others include:

- Vegetables—finely julienned, shredded, or diced and/or blanched
- Marinated artichoke hearts (without sugar)
- Steamed asparagus
- Broccoli florets
- Marinated or grilled mushrooms
- Roasted or raw bell peppers
- Scallions

(Additional protein garnishes are found in the following section.)

### HIGH PROTEIN

These recipes provide a minimum of 14 grams of protein per serving. If you wish to increase a recipe's protein content, look at the number of grams of protein in the recipe and then add the appropriate amount of protein, as indicated on the next page.

We know that protein encourages muscle development and tends to increase energy. It makes one less sluggish and promotes an overall sense of well-being in the body.

In this book you have a wide variety of healthful soups to choose from. You can also add Nutribiotic Vegetarian Rice Protein Powder to the soup: blend 1 tablespoon powder with 3 tablespoons water (to avoid clumping) before whisking it into your soup. It provides 12 grams of protein per tablespoon.

| Some Suggested Protein Enrichments | Protein per 3 oz. | Calories |
| --- | --- | --- |
| CRUMBLED BACON | 26G | 490 CAL |
| GRATED HARD-COOKED EGGS | 10.5G | 132 CAL |
| **GRATED OR CRUMBLED CHEESES, SUCH AS** | | |
| PARMESAN, GRATED | 27.5G | 335 CAL |
| CHEDDAR | 14G | 228 CAL |
| FETA | 12G | 222 CAL |
| BLUE CHEESE | 18G | 303 CAL |
| **SEEDS** | | |
| PUMPKIN SEEDS | 15.8G | 380 CAL |
| SESAME SEEDS | 14.4G | 481 CAL |
| SUNFLOWER SEEDS (DRY ROASTED) | 28G | 443 CAL |
| **PULSES** | | |
| CHICKPEAS | 4G | 75 CAL |
| LENTILS | 9G | 107 CAL |
| KIDNEY BEANS | 5G | 73 CAL |
| **NUTS** | | |
| ALMONDS, CHOPPED | 18G | 492 CAL |
| WALNUTS, CHOPPED | 21G | 516 CAL |
| **MEAT, POULTRY, AND SEAFOOD** | | |
| GRILLED OR SMOKED CHICKEN BREAST | 27G | 140 CAL |
| SHREDDED OR THINLY JULIENNED TURKEY BREAST | 26G | 115 CAL |
| GRILLED SALMON | 19G | 96 CAL |
| SPICY SHRIMP | 18G | 85 CAL |

## SMART FAT

Many of these soups comply with the American Heart Association (AHA) guidelines. Other recipes in this book can easily be modified to comply with these specifications by replacing butter and cream with olive oil and either low-fat soymilk or soy yogurt, and/or by using non-animal proteins such as tofu or vegetarian meat substitutes, as indicated. The AHA guidelines limit foods with a high saturated fat and cholesterol content. They suggest that saturated fat be limited to 10 percent or less of the total fat of a recipe serving.

Although there is no precise basis for selecting a target level for dietary cholesterol intake for all individuals, the AHA recommends <300 mg on average. By limiting cholesterol intake from foods with a high content of animal fats, individuals can also meet the dietary guidelines for saturated fat intake. This target can be readily achieved, even with periodic consumption of eggs and shellfish.

People are interested in the kinds of fats they eat today, including saturated and trans-fatty acids. Smart fats encourage the body to function optimally and may be necessary for improving brain cognition. Smart fats are healthy oils like olive, walnut, and flax. DHA omega 3-rich eggs are also good sources of smart fats.

Joanna uses olive oil in most of her recipes. This is *the* oil of choice. To add extra omega 3s to your soup, drizzle a little walnut oil onto a finished soup before serving. Each tablespoon of walnut oil adds 140 calories.

## LOW CALORIE

These recipes provide 450 calories or less per serving. When trying to lose weight, it will help to first determine your Body Mass Index (BMI). This is a measure of healthy weight. It is determined by multiplying your weight by 700, then dividing that number by your height in inches twice. A BMI from 19 to 25 is considered healthy, while someone with a BMI between 25 and 30 would be considered overweight. Anything above 30 is considered obese. (BMI equals a person's weight in kilograms divided by height in meters squared. BMI = $kg/m^2$.)

To calculate your BMI, go to http://www.consumer.gov/weightloss/bmi.htm

## VEGETARIAN OR VEGAN

Vegetarian recipes are made without proteins from animal sources, including beef, chicken, fish, and eggs. For vegans, or anyone whose diet excludes dairy products like milk and cheese, I have included substitutions, where appropriate.

## The Role of Fiber

The basic need of fiber may be 30–40 grams per day. Soluble fibers (notably beta-glucan and pectin) modestly reduce total cholesterol level as well as the "bad" LDL cholesterol level beyond those achieved by a diet low in saturated fat and cholesterol. Additionally, dietary fiber may promote satiety by slowing gastric emptying and helping to control calorie intake and body weight.

Grains, vegetables, fruits, legumes, and nuts are good sources of fiber. According to the American Heart Association, diets high in total carbohydrate (e.g., >60% of energy) can lead to elevated triglycerides and reduced HDL cholesterol, effects that may be associated with increased risk for cardiovascular disease. These changes may be lessened with diets high in fiber, in which carbohydrate is derived largely from unprocessed whole foods.

Many of the recipes in *Soup for Every Body* are excellent sources of fiber.

*An old-fashioned vegetable soup, without any enhancement, is a more powerful anticarcinogen than any known medicine.*

— James Duke MD (U.S.D.A.)

# vegetable soups

# Jerusalem Artichoke Soup with Marinated Tofu

*I originally tasted this delicate ivory-colored soup in Helsinki, Finland, in the kitchen of Jarmo Vähä-Savo, the executive chef of G. W. Sundmans. This elegant restaurant is located in an 18th-century townhouse. Jerusalem artichokes lend an earthy—albeit subtle—taste to this frothy soup that is smartly set off by tiny cubes of tofu marinated in olive oil and thyme. Serve it hot or at room temperature. I urge you to try it.*

12 ounces Jerusalem artichokes, scrubbed and coarsely chopped

1 (4-ounce) baking potato, peeled and diced or 4 ounces firm tofu

1 medium onion, peeled and sliced

2+ cups vegetable or chicken stock

½ cup dry white wine or additional stock

½ cup heavy or light cream or soy creamer

Salt

¼ pound firm tofu, cut into tiny dice

3 tablespoons fruity extra-virgin olive oil

1 teaspoon fresh thyme leaves

SERVES 4

1. Combine the Jerusalem artichokes, potatoes, onion, stock, and wine in a large pot. (If using tofu as a thickener, do not add until later.) Cover and gently boil until the vegetables are tender, about 40–45 minutes. Transfer the vegetables and liquid (along with the tofu, if using) to the jar of an electric blender and purée until completely smooth.

2. While the vegetables cook, blend the diced tofu, olive oil, thyme, and ⅛ teaspoon salt in a bowl and let marinate.

3. Return the purée to the pan, stir in cream or soy creamer, and season to taste with salt. If you do not have 4 cups of liquid, add additional stock, then heat over medium heat until hot. Ladle into heated bowls, add a generous tablespoon of the tofu garnish in the center of each bowl, and serve.

\* Jerusalem Artichokes

Jerusalem artichokes are also known as sunchokes and topinambour. They have a lovely nutty taste and can be used both cooked and raw. Simply scrub them before using. Store in the refrigerator. They last for at least a month.

They're a perennial plant resembling but unrelated to a sunflower, and if you like them you could get a patch established in your vegetable garden.

## NUTRITIONAL INFORMATION

CALORIES 290 | CALORIES FROM FAT 150 | TOTAL FAT 17G | SATURATED FAT 5G
CHOLESTEROL 20MG | TOTAL CARBOHYDRATE 26G | DIETARY FIBER 2G
SUGARS 10G | PROTEIN 5G | VITAMIN A 4% | VITAMIN C 15% | CALCIUM 6% | IRON 20%

# Curried Asparagus Soup

*Green asparagus tips add style and color to this mildly spicy soup, while a dollop of savory whipped cream or soy yogurt is the final sophisticated accent.*

1 tablespoon vegetable oil

1 medium–large (about 6 ounces) onion, peeled and chopped

2 teaspoons mild or hot curry powder

1 (6-ounce) baking potato, peeled and diced or 6 ounces firm tofu

2 cups vegetable or chicken stock

¾ pound asparagus

¾ cup milk or soy milk

Salt

1½ tablespoons finely chopped tarragon leaves

⅓ cup heavy cream or equal parts non-dairy creamer and soy yogurt

¼ teaspoon finely grated lemon zest

1. Heat the oil in a heavy saucepan over medium heat. Add the onions and sauté until wilted, about 5–6 minutes. Stir in the curry powder, cook for 2 minutes, then add the potatoes, if using, and the stock. Bring the liquid to a boil, then reduce the heat and simmer until the potatoes are almost tender, about 10 minutes.

2. Meanwhile, break off the woody ends from the asparagus. Cut off about 1 inch of the tips and reserve. Slice the asparagus crosswise into ½-inch pieces and add them to the saucepan along with 1 tablespoon of the tarragon leaves. Partially cover and simmer until the asparagus and potatoes, if using, are tender. Transfer to the jar of an electric blender, pour in the milk or soy milk, add the tofu, if using, and purée until the soup is completely smooth, then return it to pot, and season with salt.

3. Blanch the reserved asparagus tips in boiling salted water until tender. Heat the soup until hot. Add the asparagus tips to the soup and taste to adjust seasonings. Before serving, beat the heavy cream or non-dairy creamer and soy yogurt in a small bowl into soft peaks. Fold in the remaining ½ tablespoon of tarragon, ⅛ teaspoon salt, and the lemon zest. Serve each bowl with a generous spoonful of the flavored cream.

## NUTRITIONAL INFORMATION

CALORIES 220 | CALORIES FROM FAT 120 | TOTAL FAT 14G | SATURATED FAT 6G

CHOLESTEROL 35MG | TOTAL CARBOHYDRATE 20G | DIETARY FIBER 4G

SUGARS 6G | PROTEIN 6G | VITAMIN A 35% | VITAMIN C 35% | CALCIUM 15% | IRON 15%

# Avocado Guacamole Soup

*For many of us, guacamole—the avocado dip, cum tortilla chips—is positively addicting. When those same ingredients—avocado, tomatoes, onions, and jalapeños—are smoothed with a touch of stock and sour cream, you'll discover a new pleasure. Serve it at room temperature. Of course, tortilla chips make a great garnish. To make this a main-course soup, add grilled shrimp or chicken.*

SERVES 4

2 ripe avocados, (about ½ pound each), peeled

1 large onion, peeled and quartered

2 large tomatoes, peeled and seeded

1 large clove garlic

½ cup fresh lime juice

2 teaspoons hot or mild chili powder

1 teaspoon ground cumin

1½–2 teaspoons salt or to taste

Freshly ground black pepper

1½ cups chicken or vegetable stock

½ cup sour cream
+ additional sour cream to garnish

2 tablespoons Tequila (optional)

1 small onion, peeled

½–1 jalapeño pepper, seeds and membranes removed

⅔ cup loosely packed cilantro leaves
+ additional leaves to garnish

½ tablespoon red wine vinegar

Tortilla chips, to garnish (optional)

1. Combine the avocados, large onion, 1 tomato, the garlic, lime juice, chili powder, cumin, salt, black pepper, and half of the stock in a food processor and purée until smooth. Add the remaining stock, sour cream, and Tequila, and blend. Transfer the soup to a large bowl and, if desired, chill.

2. By hand, chop the remaining tomato, small onion, jalapeño, and ⅔ cup cilantro leaves together until they are finely diced and well blended.

3. Stir the vinegar and chopped onion mixture into the soup. Ladle the soup into bowls. Garnish with a dollop of sour cream, a few cilantro leaves, and serve with tortilla chips.

## NUTRITIONAL INFORMATION

CALORIES 290 | CALORIES FROM FAT 210 | TOTAL FAT 24G | SATURATED FAT 5G

CHOLESTEROL 5MG | TOTAL CARBOHYDRATE 19G | DIETARY FIBER 8G

SUGARS 5G | PROTEIN 5G | VITAMIN A 45% | VITAMIN C 60% | CALCIUM 6% | IRON 15%

# Broccoli-Almond Soup

*For this elegant, smooth soup, toasted almonds and broccoli are puréed with chicken stock. This method was used in medieval times to thicken soups. The soup is simple yet unexpectedly sophisticated with a warm hint of coriander and white pepper.*

1 pound broccoli, large stalks peeled, chopped into small pieces

4 tablespoons unsalted butter or olive oil

1 medium onion (about 5 ounces), thinly sliced

2 ounces (about ⅓ cup) blanched almonds, toasted until lightly browned

2½–3 cups chicken or vegetable stock

1½ teaspoons ground coriander

Salt and white pepper

4 tablespoons crème fraîche, a mixture of sour cream and heavy cream, or soy yogurt (optional)

SERVES 4

1. Steam or microwave the broccoli until completely tender. Reserve 4 small florets of the cooked broccoli for the final garnish.

2. Meanwhile, heat the butter or oil in a heavy saucepan over medium heat and sauté the onion until golden brown, 5–6 minutes. Combine the broccoli, onion, and almonds in the jar of an electric blender or food processor with 2½ cups of stock, and purée until completely smooth.

3. Return the mixture to the saucepan. Stir in the coriander, salt and pepper to taste, and more stock if the soup is too thick. Heat until hot, then ladle the soup into heated bowls, garnish with a dollop of cream and a broccoli floret, and serve.

## NUTRITIONAL INFORMATION

CALORIES 280 | CALORIES FROM FAT 210 | TOTAL FAT 24G | SATURATED FAT 10G

CHOLESTEROL 40MG | TOTAL CARBOHYDRATE 13G | DIETARY FIBER 6G

SUGARS 4G | PROTEIN 8G | VITAMIN A 45% | VITAMIN C 180% | CALCIUM 10% | IRON 10%

# Velvet Carrot-Ginger Soup

*This perfectly smooth, vibrant orange-hued soup relies on only a few ingredients, so each should be the best you can find. Choose young, tender carrots, high-quality butter or fruity olive oil, and a flavorful stock. A few spoonfuls of rice, sweated with the carrots, thicken the soup into a satiny potion. It's so simple to make and is easily made in large quantities, yet it always draws raves.*

SMART FAT
LOW CALORIE
VEGETARIAN OR VEGAN

4 tablespoons unsalted butter or olive oil

1 pound young carrots, peeled and diced

½ cup finely chopped shallots

¼ cup finely chopped candied or crystallized ginger

3 tablespoons raw white rice

3+ cups chicken or vegetable stock

Salt and white pepper

3 tablespoons snipped fresh chives

SERVES 4

1. Heat the butter or oil in a heavy saucepan over medium–high heat. Stir in the carrots, shallots, ginger, and rice. Cover tightly and sweat over medium–low heat until the carrots are very tender and the rice is completely soft, about 25–30 minutes.

2. Scrape the mixture into the jar of an electric blender, add 3 cups of stock, and purée until completely smooth. Pass the soup through a fine strainer and return it to pan. Season to taste with salt and pepper, stir in the chives, and reheat until hot, adding more stock if needed. Ladle into heated soup bowls and serve.

\* To Sweat Vegetables
To sweat vegetables means to cook them in a small amount of fat in a partially or fully covered pot over low heat to soften them and intensify the flavors.

\* Candied or Crystallized Ginger
Look for candied or crystallized ginger at Asian markets rather than conventional supermarkets. It usually costs substantially less money. You can also usually buy candied ginger in natural food stores, in bulk packaging, for a reasonable price and often in smaller amounts if custom-weighed.

## NUTRITIONAL INFORMATION

CALORIES 270 | CALORIES FROM FAT 120 | TOTAL FAT 14G | SATURATED FAT 8G

CHOLESTEROL 35MG | TOTAL CARBOHYDRATE 35G | DIETARY FIBER 4G

SUGARS 19G | PROTEIN 3G | VITAMIN A 650% | VITAMIN C 25% | CALCIUM 6% | IRON 8%

# Carrot Soup with Chèvre

*Here's another easy and quick carrot soup that's also fancy enough to serve to your most discerning guests. In this version, sweet young carrots are paired with slightly salty goat cheese and tangy buttermilk to produce an exciting blend of flavors*

SERVES 8

1 tablespoon olive or vegetable oil

2 tablespoons finely chopped shallots

3 pounds trimmed young carrots, peeled and coarsely chopped

6 cups chicken or vegetable stock

3 tablespoons minced candied ginger

1 teaspoon ground mace

½ teaspoon ground allspice

1 cup buttermilk

Salt and white pepper

4 ounces mild chèvre, such as Montrachet, chilled and cut into 8 slices

Fresh chervil or parsley sprigs, for garnish

1. Heat the oil in a large heavy saucepan over medium–high heat. Add the shallots and sauté until tender and lightly colored, 4–5 minutes, stirring occasionally. Add the carrots, 3 cups of the stock, and the ginger. Cover and bring the liquid to a boil over medium–high heat. Cook until the carrots are very tender, 20–30 minutes.

2. Transfer to a food processor or the jar of an electric blender and purée until smooth. Return the purée to the saucepan. Stir in the remaining stock, the allspice, and mace, and heat until hot.

3. Whisk a cup of soup into the buttermilk to warm it, then stir the buttermilk into the soup. Season with salt and pepper to taste. Simmer over medium heat for 5 minutes. Ladle the soup into heated bowls. Place a slice of chèvre and a sprig of chervil in the center of each bowl and serve.

* Chèvre

Chèvre or goat cheese can vary dramatically in both taste and texture. Young chèvre resembles cream cheese in taste: it's mild with a crumbly texture. As it ripens, the cheese becomes smoother and more assertive tasting. In France, each town or farm is known for only one style and shape of goat cheese. American manufacturers produce several shapes and styles of chèvre. Regional cheesemakers around the country are now making lines of organic chèvre, as well as plain and those variously seasoned with cracked pepper, dill, tarragon, etc.

## NUTRITIONAL INFORMATION

CALORIES 190 | CALORIES FROM FAT 70 | TOTAL FAT 8G | SATURATED FAT 3G
CHOLESTEROL 15MG | TOTAL CARBOHYDRATE 25G | DIETARY FIBER 5G
SUGARS 17G | PROTEIN 7G | VITAMIN A 960% | VITAMIN C 25% | CALCIUM 20% | IRON 6%

# Velouté of Cauliflower

*A velouté is a rich soup or sauce thickened with a light roux—a little cooked flour and a pale stock—then enriched with egg yolks and heavy cream. In this cauliflower velouté, the subtle and elegant marriage of flavors would make a fine beginning to your most festive meal. Omit the bread or substitute Parmesan Crisps (see page 135) to keep this low carb.*

*Make sure to slowly whisk the heated stock into the eggs, so they don't scramble. When you return the eggs and soup to the pot, the mixture should barely simmer: only small bubbles should break the surface of the hot soup as it cooks. Usually this means using medium–low heat.*

SERVES 6

1 head cauliflower (approximately 1 pound cleaned), broken into florets

6 tablespoons unsalted butter

½ cup finely chopped onion

3 tablespoons all-purpose flour

4 cups chicken or vegetable stock

6 whole allspice berries

6 whole black peppercorns

1 bay leaf

2 egg yolks

⅜ cup heavy cream or soy creamer

Generous pinch freshly grated nutmeg

Salt and white pepper

Sourdough-Parmesan Crostini (page 137), optional

Snipped fresh chives, to garnish

1. Steam the cauliflower until tender, about 15–20 minutes. In the meantime, melt 2 tablespoons of the butter in a heavy skillet over medium heat. Add the onion and sauté until golden, 6–8 minutes, stirring occasionally.

2. Transfer the cauliflower and onion to the jar of an electric blender or food processor, add 1 cup of stock, and purée until smooth, scraping down the sides as needed. Return the purée to a large pot and set aside.

3. Melt 3 tablespoons of the butter in a heavy saucepan. Stir in the flour using a wooden spoon and cook over medium–low heat until the flour is golden colored, about 12–14 minutes, stirring often. Slowly whisk in the remaining stock. Add the bay leaf, allspice berries, and black peppercorns, reduce the heat to low, and simmer for 30 minutes, stirring occasionally. Strain the stock into the cauliflower purée, whisking to blend well. Soup may be done ahead to this point.

4. Just before serving, bring the soup to a simmer. Combine the egg yolks and cream in a medium-sized bowl. Slowly whisk about 1 cup of the heated

soup into the cream-yolk mixture, beating constantly to raise the temperature. Add a second cup of soup to the bowl and, when blended, return this into the soup pot. Season to taste with nutmeg, salt, and pepper.

5. Ladle the hot soup into bowls. If using, place two cheese crostini in each bowl. Sprinkle with the chives and serve.

NUTRITIONAL INFORMATION

CALORIES 310 | CALORIES FROM FAT 200 | TOTAL FAT 22G | SATURATED FAT 12G
CHOLESTEROL 125MG | TOTAL CARBOHYDRATE 22G | DIETARY FIBER 3G
SUGARS 3G | PROTEIN 7G | VITAMIN A 15% | VITAMIN C 60% | CALCIUM 10% | IRON 8%

# Triple Mushroom Soup

*This combination of fresh white and baby bella mushrooms, along with rehy-drated dried shiitakes, is sure to please. Reducing the water used to soak the dried shiitakes down to ½ cup and then using it in the soup adds a more intense mushroom flavor to this soup.*

SERVES 4

2 cups hot water

2 ounces dried shiitake mushrooms

½ pound white mushrooms, wiped and trimmed

½ pound baby bella mushrooms, wiped and trimmed

2 tablespoons unsalted butter or olive oil

1 tablespoon vegetable oil

2 tablespoons minced shallots

2 cups vegetable or chicken stock

1 bay leaf

4 sprigs fresh thyme or 1 teaspoon dried thyme leaves

Salt and freshly ground pepper

½ pint crème fraîche, sour cream, or plain cow's milk or soy yogurt

Freshly snipped chives or thinly sliced scallions, to garnish

1. Pour the hot water over the dried shiitakes and soak until softened. Strain the mushrooms in a strainer lined with moistened paper towels, reserving the liquid. Bring the liquid to a boil over high heat and reduce to ½ cup. Reserve. Remove and discard the mushrooms' woody stems and cut the mushrooms into thin slices.

2. Finely chop the white and baby bella mushrooms. If you do this in a food processor, pulse until finely chopped. Do not let the machine run.

3. Heat the butter and oil over medium heat in a deep saucepan. Cook the shallots until they are wilted and golden, about 5 minutes. Add the chopped fresh mushrooms and cook until they have given up their liquid, stirring often.

4. Pour in the stock, add the bay leaf, thyme, salt, and plenty of pepper along with the sliced shiitakes and the reserved mushroom liquid. Partially cover and simmer for 15 minutes. Remove the bay leaf. Stir in the crème fraîche and simmer to heat through. Ladle into heated bowls, sprinkle with chives or scallions, and serve.

## NUTRITIONAL INFORMATION

CALORIES 280 | CALORIES FROM FAT 190 | TOTAL FAT 21G | SATURATED FAT 11G

CHOLESTEROL 40MG | TOTAL CARBOHYDRATE 17G | DIETARY FIBER 7G

SUGARS 2G | PROTEIN 8G | VITAMIN A 15% | VITAMIN C 6% | CALCIUM 6% | IRON 10%

# Wild Mushroom Soup with Sage, Dried Apples & Hazelnuts

*A couple of years ago, I was asked to judge a hazelnut recipe contest in Istanbul, Turkey—not a bad reason to visit this fascinating country. When I returned, I wrote a number of articles about the nut and talked with American chefs who regularly use it. This exquisitely flavorful and subtly nuanced soup is from Chef Cory Schrieber of Wildwood Restaurant in Portland, Oregon.*

*Although Turkey is the world's leading producer of hazelnuts, they also grow in America's Pacific Northwest. The region is also recognized as a source for superb wild mushrooms. This soup blends chanterelles, hazelnuts, apples, and potatoes into a lush soup that fills the mouth with its velvety texture and robust taste.*

SERVES 8

2 tablespoons unsalted butter or olive oil

2 small ribs celery, trimmed and chopped

1 parsnip, peeled and chopped

1 yellow onion, peeled and chopped

1 small leek, white part only, washed and chopped

2–3 teaspoons salt

1 tablespoon water

1 pound fresh crimini or chanterelle mushrooms, trimmed, wiped, and thinly sliced

4 cups chicken or vegetable stock

½ cup apple cider

1 large Yukon Gold or russet potato, peeled and chopped or 1 cup puréed tofu

½ tablespoon fennel seeds, toasted and ground

¼ cup apple brandy, hard apple cider, or an additional ¼ cup apple cider

1–1½ teaspoons apple cider vinegar

Freshly ground black pepper

½ cup chopped dried apples

½ cup hazelnuts, toasted, skinned, and finely chopped

3–4 fresh sage leaves, sliced crosswise into thin strips

1. Melt 1 tablespoon of butter in a large heavy pot over low heat. Stir in the celery, parsnips, onion, fennel, leek, and about 1 teaspoon of salt. Sauté for 5 minutes, add the water, and stir in about a quarter of the mushrooms. Cover, and cook, stirring occasionally, for 20 minutes, or until the vegetables begin to soften. Add the stock and cider and bring to a boil. Add the potatoes and fennel seeds, reduce the heat, and simmer until the potatoes are soft, 20–25 minutes.

2. Transfer the soup in batches to the jar of an electric blender and purée until smooth. Pour through a fine strainer back into the pan.

3. Before serving, heat the remaining butter over medium heat in a large heavy pot. Add the remaining mushrooms, partially cover, and sauté until soft, about 8 minutes. Add the brandy or cider, pepper, remaining salt, and simmer for 5 minutes. Pour in the puréed soup and heat until warm.

4. Serve each portion with about ½ tablespoon chopped apple, 1 tablespoon chopped hazelnuts, and a generous pinch of sage leaves.

* Hazelnut Facts

Roasting hazelnuts increases their flavor and improves their crunchy texture. Although available "natural" or "roasted," natural kernels have the longest shelf life. Professionals says that although it is easy to roast them, cleaned nuts are a great time saver and definitely worth the money.

To roast natural hazelnuts, spread whole nuts in a single layer on a baking sheet and bake at 275°F for 15 to 20 minutes. To remove the skins, briskly rub with a rough cloth while nuts are still warm.

Store hazelnuts in a tightly sealed container in the refrigerator or freezer to maintain the highest quality of flavor and texture. Allow hazelnuts to warm to room temperature in unopened containers before using to prevent mold and rancidity. Refrigerated hazelnuts can be kept for up to one year. Frozen hazelnuts can be kept for up to two years.

Oregonians call hazelnuts filberts. Some people believe the name originally referred to August 22, the feast day of Saint Philibert, in England, when the nuts were first harvested; others believe it was a corruption of the words "full beard," referring to the long, draped that cover the shell.

Domestic hazelnuts grow larger, but Turkish nuts are easier to skin after roasting.

**NUTRITIONAL INFORMATION**

CALORIES 190 | CALORIES FROM FAT 120 | TOTAL FAT 13G | SATURATED FAT 2.5G
CHOLESTEROL 10MG | TOTAL CARBOHYDRATE 16G | DIETARY FIBER 4G
SUGARS 2G | PROTEIN 5G | VITAMIN A 2% | VITAMIN C 15% | CALCIUM 4% | IRON 10%

# Hearty Onion Soup

*For onion soup that lingers in your mind long after the last spoonful is gone, try this: caramelized onions puréed with Riesling wine, sherry, and chicken stock. It's as satisfying as the original French version, typically made with beef stock, but accessible to everyone, including vegetarians. Gruyère crostini are a contemporary interpretation of the typical (often heavy) cheese topping.*

SERVES 4–6

5 + 1 tablespoons unsalted butter or vegetable oil

2½ + ½ pounds yellow onions, peeled and thinly sliced

½ cup Riesling wine or white grape juice

4 cups chicken or vegetable stock

½ cup medium sherry or ¼ cup apple juice concentrate

Salt and white pepper to taste

8–12 thin slices narrow French baguette, lightly toasted

1 clove garlic, split

2 tablespoons olive oil

1½ cups finely shredded Gruyère cheese or soy cheese

1. Melt 5 tablespoons of butter in a large heavy casserole. Add the 2½ pounds of onions and sauté over medium–high heat until soft and richly browned, 25–30 minutes. Stir and scrape the pan often to prevent burning.

2. While the onions are cooking, heat the remaining tablespoon of butter in a skillet and sauté the remaining ½ pound of sliced onions over medium heat until soft and golden brown. Set aside.

3. Add the Riesling and ½ cup of the stock to the casserole and bring to a boil, stirring up all browned bits. Scrape the mixture into a food processor or the jar of an electric blender and purée until smooth. Return the mixture to the casserole, add the remaining stock, sherry, salt and pepper, and simmer for 5 minutes. Stir in the sautéed onions and keep warm over medium–low heat.

4. Rub the toasted bread slices with garlic and brush with oil. Put them on a cookie sheet, sprinkle on the cheese, and run them under a broiler until the cheese is melted and lightly brown.

5. Ladle 1 cup of soup into each heated bowl, add 2 crostini, and serve at once.

## NUTRITIONAL INFORMATION

CALORIES 560 | CALORIES FROM FAT 330 | TOTAL FAT 37G | SATURATED FAT 19G

CHOLESTEROL 95 MG | TOTAL CARBOHYDRATE 32G | DIETARY FIBER 5G

SUGARS 6G | PROTEIN 22G | VITAMIN A 25% | VITAMIN C 25% | CALCIUM 60% | IRON 8%

# Roasted Parsnip Soup
# with Diced Fennel

*When the humble parsnip is slowly sweated until tender and lightly browned, it imparts a sweet, earthy flavor to this satisfying soup. The fennel bulb is cut into equal-sized cubes, or diced, then sautéed and stirred into the soup before serving. It adds a crunchy accent, while the fronds add visual appeal. A tiny glass of dry sherry is an ideal complement to serve with this refined soup.*

3 tablespoons unsalted butter or olive oil

2 pounds medium parsnips, peeled, cut in quarters lengthwise and coarsely chopped

6 cups chicken or vegetable stock

½ cup light cream or soy creamer

¼–½ cup dry sherry (optional)

Salt to taste

¾ cup finely diced fennel bulb; reserve some fennel fronds for garnish

SERVES 6–8

1. Heat 2 tablespoons of the butter or oil in a large skillet over medium–high heat. Add the parsnips, turning to coat with the butter. Partially cover the pan and sweat the parsnips over medium–low heat until they are tender and lightly browned, about 45 minutes, stirring occasionally. Pour about a cup of stock into the pan, stirring up any browned bits. Scrape the parsnips into the jar of an electric blender and purée until completely smooth. Return to a saucepan.

2. Add the remaining stock, the light cream, sherry, if using, and salt. Simmer until hot.

3. Meanwhile, melt the remaining tablespoon of butter in a small skillet over medium–high heat. When hot, stir in the diced fennel and quickly sauté until lightly colored, 45–50 seconds. Ladle the soup into heated bowls, add a heaping tablespoon of fennel in the center of each bowl and a couple of small fennel fronds to garnish, and serve at once.

\* Soup Duets

Two soups served together make a dramatic presentation. For these duets to work, both soups should be the same consistency, the flavors should complement one another, and they should be different colors. There are two methods to do this. You can simultaneously pour equal amounts of the soups into opposite sides of a flat soup bowl (it doesn't matter if the line swerves a bit). Or, fill a warmed soup bowl with about ¾ cup of one soup, then pour about ¼ cup of the second soup in the center of the bowl. If necessary, thin one soup to match the consistency of its partner.

SOME SUGGESTED PAIRINGS:
Roasted Parsnip Soup with Diced Fennel and Simple Butternut Squash Soup with Apple & Walnuts

Leek & Potato Soup (without the mussels) and Broccoli-Almond Soup

Creamy Pumpkin Soup (with or without the bacon) and Roasted Red Pepper & Paprika Soup

Peach Soup with Blueberries & Peach Sorbet and Minted Watermelon Soup

## NUTRITIONAL INFORMATION

CALORIES 200 | CALORIES FROM FAT 80 | TOTAL FAT 9G | SATURATED FAT 4.5G

CHOLESTEROL 20MG | TOTAL CARBOHYDRATE 24G | DIETARY FIBER 6G

SUGARS <1G | PROTEIN 3G | VITAMIN A 6% | VITAMIN C 35% | CALCIUM 6% | IRON 4%

# Three "P" Soup—Peas, Prosciutto & Parmesan Cheese

*This soup was inspired by one of my favorite pasta dishes—Pasta Tre "P"—in which prosciutto, peas, and Parmesan are combined in a creamy sauce. I serve it as often for dinner parties as family meals. Unless it's late spring when young peas can be found in the market, I rely on tiny frozen peas. The vibrant green soup is served with a delicious Parmesan-Black Pepper Crisp either hot or at room temperature.*

SERVES 6

8 tablespoons (1 stick) unsalted butter or olive oil

⅓ cup finely chopped shallots

1 small head Boston or Bibb lettuce, washed, cored, shaken of excess water and cut into thin strips

2 (16-ounce) packages frozen "petite" peas, defrosted

2 teaspoons salt or to taste

2 teaspoons sugar or to taste

4 cups chicken or vegetarian stock

1 cup light cream

4 ounces prosciutto or vegetarian bacon, cut into fine dice

Parmesan-Black Pepper Crisps (page 135)

1. Heat the butter or oil in a large saucepan over medium heat. Add the shallots and cook until translucent, about 3–4 minutes. Add the lettuce and peas—reserving about ½ cup for the final garnish—and salt and sugar. Cover the pan and cook gently for 10 minutes.

2. Transfer the peas to a food processor or the jar of an electric blender and purée until smooth. Do this in batches. Reserve any liquid in the pan not used to purée the peas. Pass the peas through a fine strainer to eliminate the pea skins. Return the mixture to the pan.

3. Stir in the stock, cream, and prosciutto and cook over medium heat for 5–7 minutes.

4. Meanwhile, prepare the Parmesan-Black Pepper Crisps.

5. Ladle the soup into heated bowls. Serve with Parmesan-Black Pepper Crisps.

## NUTRITIONAL INFORMATION

CALORIES 410 | CALORIES FROM FAT 240 | TOTAL FAT 27G | SATURATED FAT 16G

CHOLESTEROL 85MG | TOTAL CARBOHYDRATES 27 G | DIETARY FIBER 8G

SUGARS 10G | PROTEIN 16G | VITAMIN A 40% | VITAMIN C 1,000% | CALCIUM 10% | IRON 15%

# Roasted Red Pepper & Paprika Soup

*Amelia Hunt left Manhattan and a successful marketing career for life at Falls Brook Farm in Lyme, Connecticut, when she married farmer Michael Newburg in 2002. Long Island Sound is just out of sight from the rolling landscape of the farm. The idea to dry and grind their organic Hungarian peppers to make paprika came from regular visitors to their on-site farm stand.*

*"At first I just borrowed a dryer and used a coffee grinder." Now Hunt uses a small commercial dryer for her paprika production. "It takes about twenty peppers to produce an ounce of paprika," she explains. "I have to seed, quarter, and dry them. They become intensely fragrant before I grind them." Amelia Hunt serves this bright vermilion-colored soup hot or cold, depending on the season. Bottled roasted red peppers could be substituted to save time, and the variety and number of chile peppers should be chosen for heat, according to your taste. Use plastic gloves when handling fresh chiles.*

SERVES 4

2 pounds (about 4 large) red bell peppers (see note)

1 medium onion, peeled and chopped

1 tablespoons olive oil

2 large cloves garlic, minced

1–2 fresh red chiles, such as jalapeños, seeds and membranes removed, sliced

½ teaspoon hot or sweet paprika

4 cups chicken or vegetable broth

½ pound red potatoes, peeled and diced

1 bouquet garni (including a fresh bay leaf, 2 sprigs flat-leaf parsley, or chervil, 2 sprigs thyme or marjoram, and 1 rib celery with leaves tied with string for easy removal, or dried herbs tied in a cheesecloth square)

Salt

1 tablespoon fresh thyme leaves, chopped

2 tablespoons half-and-half or heavy cream (optional)

1. Halve, seed, and grill the red peppers over a high flame until blackened. Place in a brown paper bag and close. When cool enough to handle, remove as much of the charred skin as possible. Blot on paper towels, then coarsely chop. Set aside.

2. Heat the oil in a large heavy casserole over medium heat. Add the onions, garlic, and chilies, cover, and sweat until soft, but not brown, 10–15 minutes. Add the paprika and cook another minute. Add the reserved bell peppers, stock, potatoes, and bouquet garni, and simmer until potatoes are soft, about 20 minutes.

3. Remove the bouquet garni, then transfer mixture to the jar of an electric blender, food processor, or use an immersion blender to purée the soup until smooth. Return the soup to the pot, season to taste with salt, stir in the fresh thyme and cream, if using, and heat until hot or let cool to room temperature. Garnish with croutons if served hot or sour cream if served cold.

NOTE: If you purchase roasted peppers, you will need about 1 pound of pepper fillets after the seeds and membranes have been removed, or 1–1½ (16-ounce) jars of peppers. This way it's easy to make enough to feed a crowd.

## NUTRITIONAL INFORMATION

CALORIES 170 | CALORIES FROM FAT 50 | TOTAL FAT 5G | SATURATED FAT 0.5G
CHOLESTEROL 0MG | TOTAL CARBOHYDRATE 27G | DIETARY FIBER 6G
SUGARS 6G | PROTEIN 5G | VITAMIN A 35% | VITAMIN C 360% | CALCIUM 4% | IRON 10%

* Making Your Own Fresh-Ground Hungarian Paprika

If you'd like to make your own fresh-ground Hungarian paprika, there many sources for purchasing the seeds on the Internet. One, Johnny's Selected Seeds (www.johnnyseeds.com), sells seeds called Hungarian Boldog Spice. Once you grow the peppers, dry them and then grind batches in a mortar and pestle as needed. They do indeed make wonderful paprika.

* Proliferating Peppers

There are so many varieties of chiles available these days, not just in gourmet markets but from specialty seed companies for home gardening, representing a wide range of heat. For example, anaheim, anchos, and poblanos are relatively mild and sweet, whereas jalapeños are relatively hot. They are the best known hot pepper in the United States today, and are a staple for Tex-Mex dishes like salsas, nachos, and pico de gallo.

Although some retail stores try to indicate the general degree of heat contained in the different varieties and shapes of chile peppers, a basic rule of thumb is that that smaller the top of the pepper, the hotter it is. Also remember that lot of the heat is contained in the membranes and seeds, which is why it's important to remove these.

# Country Potato Soup with Rapini

*Tangy, robust, and full of flavor, this chunky, creamy yellow potato soup is simmered with assertive-tasting rapini and then topped with Cheddar cheese. It's unpretentious, nourishing, and comforting but only for lovers of rapini, also called broccoli rabe. Serve with a crusty chunk of bread. Substitute white potatoes if you cannot find yellow potatoes.*

SERVES 8

1 tablespoon olive oil

1 large onion, peeled and thinly sliced

2 large cloves garlic, chopped

4 cups vegetable or chicken stock

2 pounds Yukon Gold or other yellow-fleshed potatoes, peeled and coarsely chopped

¼ teaspoon red pepper flakes

1 (12-ounce) bunch rapini, thick stems discarded and cut into 1-inch pieces

2 cups buttermilk

Salt and freshly ground black pepper

1½–2 cups shredded medium or sharp Cheddar cheese or soy cheese

1. Heat the oil in a large heavy saucepan over medium–high heat until hot. Stir in the onion and cook until soft and light brown, about 5 minutes, stirring occasionally. Stir in the garlic and cook until soft, 1 to 2 minutes. Add the stock, potatoes, and red pepper flakes. Partially cover and gently boil until the potatoes are tender, 15–18 minutes. Add the rapini and cook just until tender, 2–3 minutes.

2. Transfer the soup to the food processor and pulse until it is chunky–smooth. Scrape the mixture back into saucepan and heat until hot. Stir in the buttermilk and bring the soup just to a simmer. Do not boil. If it is too thick, thin it with a little water. Season with salt and pepper.

3. Ladle the soup into wide soup bowls. Sprinkle on the cheese and serve.

* Taming Rapini

Rapini is a member of the mustard family (Cruciferae or Brassicaceae) that includes kohlrabi, brussels sprouts, kale, and dandelion greens. These nutritious vegetables tend to be assertive tasting. You can soften their bite by boiling them for 5 minutes in salted water before sautéing or using them in stir-fry dishes.

## NUTRITIONAL INFORMATION

CALORIES 240 | CALORIES FROM FAT 90 | TOTAL FAT 10G | SATURATED FAT 5G

CHOLESTEROL 25MG | TOTAL CARBOHYDRATE 27G | DIETARY FIBER 4G

SUGARS 5G | PROTEIN 12G | VITAMIN A 120% | VITAMIN C 60% | CALCIUM 30% | IRON 15%

# Sautéed Salsify Soup with White Truffle Oil

*Salsify is a lovely creamy-colored vegetable that is also known as oyster plant for its delicate taste of oysters when cooked. This simple but exquisite soup, with a drizzle of luxurious white truffle oil, reveals why Europeans adore this vegetable that is sadly underappreciated in America. The edible roots look like wild carrots or long, thin parsnips. The easily peeled skin is pale beige. Their Italian cousin, scorzonera, has a black skin.*

*I have seen salsify in some gourmet produce markets and also purchased the seeds and grown my own.*

1½ pounds salsify

2 tablespoons unsalted butter or olive oil

1 teaspoon vegetable oil

3 cups vegetable stock

2 sprigs fresh thyme

⅓ cup light cream or soy creamer

Salt and white pepper

White truffle oil

SERVES 4

1. Peel the salsify with a potato peeler and cut it into 2-inch pieces. Do this just before cooking so the vegetable does not discolor. Heat the butter or oil in a large, heavy, deep skillet over medium heat. Add the salsify, shaking to coat evenly, partially cover, and sweat for 40 minutes, shaking the pan occasionally. Uncover the pan, raise the heat to medium–high, and cook until the pieces begin to turn light brown, about 10 minutes, shaking the pan often.

2. Add the stock and thyme to the pan, bring the liquid to a boil, re-cover, and cook until completely tender, about 20 minutes.

3. Remove and discard the thyme. Transfer the salsify and liquid to the jar of an electric blender and purée until completely smooth. Return the soup to the pan, stir in the cream, season to taste with salt and white pepper, and heat until hot.

4. Ladle the soup into bowls, drizzle about 1 teaspoon of truffle oil into each bowl, and serve.

## NUTRITIONAL INFORMATION

CALORIES 180 | CALORIES FROM FAT 130 | TOTAL FAT 15G | SATURATED FAT 7G

CHOLESTEROL 30MG | TOTAL CARBOHYDRATE 10G | DIETARY FIBER 4G

SUGARS 4G | PROTEIN 5G | VITAMIN A 8% | VITAMIN C 130% | CALCIUM 6% | IRON 4%

# Sweet Potato, Caramelized Onion & Apple Cider Soup

*When an autumn chill is in the air, this hardy marriage of sweet potatoes, caramelized onions, fresh apple cider, and a dash of bourbon will warm you up in a hurry. Chopped walnuts and shredded sage leaves complement the soup's color, texture, and taste.*

*Baking the sweet potatoes ahead of time in the same oven while baking regular white potatoes for dinner—or other foods requiring about the same temperature—is both energy-efficient and a time saver when you're ready to prepare this soup.*

1½ pounds sweet potatoes or yams

2 tablespoons unsalted butter or olive oil

2 large onions, peeled and thinly sliced

1 cup fresh apple cider

¼ cup bourbon or 1 tablespoon unsulphured molasses + 3 tablespoons water

2 cups chicken or vegetable stock

Salt and white pepper

2 tablespoon finely chopped walnuts, lightly toasted

1 tablespoon finely shredded fresh sage leaves

SERVES 4–6

1. Preheat the oven to 400°F. Bake the potatoes until tender, about 1 hour. Set aside to cool, then peel. While the potatoes are baking, heat the butter in a large saucepan over medium–high heat. Stir in the onions, adjust the heat to medium, and sauté until golden brown and very tender, about 20–25 minutes, stirring often.

2. Transfer the onions, sweet potatoes, and apple cider to a food processor and purée until smooth.

3. Return the purée to the pan, and stir in the bourbon or molasses. Add the stock to the purée and bring to a boil, then reduce heat and simmer for 3–4 minutes. Season to taste with salt and pepper.

4. Ladle the soup into heated bowls, sprinkle a small amount of chopped walnuts and shredded sage leaves in the center of each bowl, and serve.

## NUTRITIONAL INFORMATION

CALORIES 220 | CALORIES FROM FAT 70 | TOTAL FAT 7G | SATURATED FAT 2.5G

CHOLESTEROL 10MG | TOTAL CARBOHYDRATE 27G | DIETARY FIBER <1G

SUGARS 2G | PROTEIN 4G | VITAMIN A 4% | VITAMIN C 4% | CALCIUM 2% | IRON 4%

# Creamy Pumpkin Soup with Bacon

*Serve this soup, inspired by Sally Kofke's recipe, with grilled cheese sandwiches for an informal lunch. Or, to elevate it, sauté cubes of foie gras and stir them into the soup at the very last minute.*

SERVES 8

4 slices thick-cut smoked bacon or vegetarian bacon, cut into thin strips

Vegetable oil

1 large onion, peeled and finely chopped

2 cups canned pumpkin purée

1 large baking potato, peeled and coarsely chopped

3 cups chicken and vegetable stock

3 cups water

½ teaspoon ground cinnamon

¼ teaspoon freshly grated nutmeg

Few dashes hot pepper sauce

1 cup heavy or light cream or soy creamer (optional)

Salt and freshly ground black pepper

2 scallions including green parts, thinly sliced

Chili-Crusted Pumpkin Seeds (page 138), to garnish (optional)

4 ounces foie gras, to garnish (optional), instead of the pumpkin seeds

1. Cook the bacon in a large heavy pot over medium heat until the fat is rendered and the bacon is crisp. Remove to a paper towel and set aside. Add oil to the pot, if needed, to have about 2 tablespoons of fat in the pan. Add the onion and sauté over medium heat until it is softened and translucent, about 5 minutes, stirring occasionally.

2. Stir in the pumpkin, potato, chicken stock, and water, and bring to a boil. Cover, adjust the heat so the liquid is simmering, and cook until the potatoes are tender, about 30 minutes.

3. Prepare the Chili-Crusted Pumpkin Seeds, if using.

4. Transfer the vegetables and liquid to the jar of an electric blender and purée until smooth. This will have to be done in batches. Return the soup to the pan, add the cream, if using, and season with cinnamon, nutmeg, pepper sauce, and salt and pepper. Reheat and taste to adjust the seasonings.

5. Crumble the reserved bacon. Ladle the soup into heated bowls. Garnish with the bacon, scallions, and Chili-Crusted Pumpkin Seeds, if using, and serve.

## NUTRITIONAL INFORMATION

CALORIES 190 | CALORIES FROM FAT 130 | TOTAL FAT 15G | SATURATED FAT 8G
CHOLESTEROL 45MG | TOTAL CARBOHYDRATE 11G | DIETARY FIBER 3G
SUGARS 3G | PROTEIN 4G | VITAMIN A 280% | VITAMIN C 15% | CALCIUM 4% | IRON 6%

* Foie Gras

If using foie gras, you will need 2 (2-ounce) slices of fresh duck foie gras, available in the refrigerated section of specialty food stores or butchers. Or, you can order it on the web from D'Artagnan (www.dartagnan.com). Blot dry on paper towel. Heat a skillet over high heat until hot. Season the foie gras with sea salt and sauté for 1 minute per side. Remove, cut into cubes, and immediately stir them into the hot soup.

# Simple Butternut Squash Soup with Apples & Walnuts

*This lovely, pale butterscotch-colored soup is luscious tasting but oh-so-quick to make. The secret to its rich flavor is toasted walnuts, unsweetened applesauce, and light cream all puréed in the blender. To further simplify the recipe, you could use frozen puréed butternut squash, but I think oven-roasting imparts a richer, sweeter taste to the squash.*

SERVES 6

1 tablespoon unsalted butter or olive oil

1 medium onion, peeled and chopped

1½ cups butternut squash, fresh or frozen peeled chunks, cooked (see note) or puréed cooked squash

3 cups vegetable, chicken, or duck stock (see variation on next page)

1 cup unsweetened applesauce or 1½ cups diced peeled apple cooked with the onion (above)

¼ cup toasted walnut pieces + 2 tablespoons toasted pieces, finely chopped, to garnish

½ teaspoon ground mace

1 cup light cream or soy creamer

Salt and ground white pepper

2 tablespoons finely chopped fresh chervil leaves or flat-leaf parsley

1. Heat the butter in a medium-sized heavy pot over medium–high heat. Add the onions and diced apple, if using, and sauté until tender and golden colored, 5–6 minutes. Scrape into the jar of an electric blender. Add the squash, 1 cup of the stock, the applesauce, ¼ cup walnut pieces, and mace, and purée until completely smooth. Return to the pot.

2. Whisk in the cream and the remaining stock. Season to taste with salt and pepper. Bring to a boil, then simmer for 2 minutes. Stir in the chervil, ladle the soup into bowls, garnish each bowl with about a teaspoon of walnuts, and serve.

NOTE: Cook peeled and cut-up chunks of butternut squash on an oiled baking sheet in a 400°F oven, turning until all sides are lightly browned and the squash is tender, about 45–50 minutes. Or bake whole squash as detailed in Southwestern Butternut Squash Soup (page 50). Then proceed with the recipe.

### Butternut Squash & Duck Soup

For a more festive soup, prepare the soup with duck and duck stock. If you have about 12 ounces of leftover cooked duck meat, cut the meat into small cubes and stir into the soup before serving to warm them up. It adds 13.5g protein, 64g fat, 51g cholesterol per serving.

Or, buy a duck breast. Remove the skin, cut it into small squares, and sauté in a heavy skillet over medium–low heat to render all the fat. Remove the "cracklings" with a slotted spoon to paper towels, blot well, and season with salt. Gently poach the duck in a little stock until it is just cooked through. Remove, cool, and shred or dice. Use duck stock (page 147) to prepare this recipe and garnish with those divine cracklings at the last minute.

**NUTRITIONAL INFORMATION**

CALORIES 180 | CALORIES FROM FAT 120 | TOTAL FAT 14G | SATURATED FAT 6G
CHOLESTEROL 30MG | TOTAL CARBOHYDRATE 13G | DIETARY FIBER 2G
SUGARS 2G | PROTEIN 4G | VITAMIN A 45% | VITAMIN C 10% | CALCIUM 6% | IRON 2%

＊ A Taste of Chervil
Beautiful chervil leaves look like feathery carrot tops. They are related. Its mildly sweet, subtly licorice taste is lost if cooked for more than a minute or so. Add it at the very end of your cooking just before serving. Don't use the dried version. (It tastes like musty cardboard.)

# Southwestern Butternut Squash Soup

*This robust Southwestern-flavored soup is a favorite cold-weather lunch or simple supper. It's rich in texture and flavor, especially with the addition of spicy chocolate-based mole paste, available at Mexican food stores. To make it as tempting to look at as it tastes, drizzle sour cream, plain yogurt, or soy yogurt decoratively on the top and shower with chopped cilantro and sliced scallions.*

SERVES 6–8

1 (3-pound) butternut squash, split, seeds and fibers removed

1 tablespoon vegetable oil

1 cup finely chopped onion

1 tablespoon minced garlic

1 medium-sized red and green bell pepper, seeds and membranes removed, and finely chopped

3 tablespoons prepared dark mole paste

2 teaspoons ground coriander

2 teaspoons ground cumin

4 cups chicken or vegetable stock

Salt and freshly ground black pepper

1 (8-ounce) container sour cream, plain yogurt, or soy yogurt

Chopped cilantro leaves and sliced scallions, to garnish

1. Preheat the oven to 350°F.

2. Place the squash, cut side down, on a lightly oiled baking pan and bake until soft, about 45–55 minutes. Remove from the oven and, when cool enough to handle, scrape the flesh into a bowl. Mash with a fork until more or less smooth. You should have about 3 cups of squash.

3. Heat the oil in a large saucepan over medium heat. Sauté the onions until translucent, 5–6 minutes. Add the garlic, cook for 30 seconds, then stir in the peppers, mole paste, coriander, cumin, stock, and squash. Bring to a boil, then reduce the heat to medium, and continue cooking for about 5 minutes longer. Season to taste with salt and plenty of pepper.

4. Fill a clean plastic squeeze-bottle with the sour cream or yogurt. Ladle the soup into wide, heated bowls. Squeeze the sour cream or yogurt onto the soup in a crosshatch or squiggle pattern. Sprinkle on the cilantro and scallions. Serve hot or at room temperature.

## NUTRITIONAL INFORMATION

CALORIES 140 | CALORIES FROM FAT 35 | TOTAL FAT 4G | SATURATED FAT 1G
CHOLESTEROL <5MG | TOTAL CARBOHYDRATE 25G | DIETARY FIBER 7G
SUGARS 9G | PROTEIN 4G | VITAMIN A 240% | VITAMIN C 100% | CALCIUM 15% | IRON 10%

\* Mole Paste
  Mole paste is sold in Hispanic grocery stores and some supermarkets.

# Dilled Cream of Yellow & Green Squash Soup

*Foods with appealing textures and colors tempt us long before we ever taste them. This sunny soup is quick and easy to make. It will satisfy your taste-buds, as well. The "cream" in this soup is actually low-fat buttermilk, puréed vegetables, and rice. Serve it hot or at room temperature.*

SERVES 6

2 tablespoons vegetable oil

½ cup minced shallots

1½ pounds mixed yellow and green squash (summer squash and zucchini), cut into ½-inch slices

½ pound tender young carrots, peeled and thinly sliced

3 tablespoons raw white rice

4 cups chicken or vegetable stock

⅓–½ cup chopped fresh dill + tiny sprigs to garnish

1¼ cups buttermilk

2 teaspoons ground coriander

Salt and white pepper

1. Heat the oil in a large, heavy saucepan over medium heat. When hot, stir in the shallots and cook until translucent, 3 minutes. Stir in the squashes, carrots, rice, and stock. Bring to a boil, cover, and adjust the heat down so the liquid is simmering. Cook until the rice is tender, about 20 minutes, stirring occasionally.

2. Transfer the mixture to a food processor and purée until almost smooth. Return it to pan, heat until hot, then stir in the dill, buttermilk, coriander, salt, and pepper to taste. Do not allow the soup to reboil or it will curdle. Serve at once or let it cool to room temperature. Ladle into bowls and garnish with tiny sprigs of dill.

\* Buttermilk

Buttermilk has 1½ percent milk fat or less and only 4 grams of fat in an 8-ounce serving. Compared with heavy cream, its smart nutritional count and refreshing tang make it a useful ingredient in creamy soups. However, try not to buy ½ percent buttermilk, because it tastes very thin in soups.

## NUTRITIONAL INFORMATION

CALORIES 130 | CALORIES FROM FAT 50 | TOTAL FAT 6G | SATURATED FAT 0.5G
CHOLESTEROL 0MG | TOTAL CARBOHYDRATE 17G | DIETARY FIBER 3G
SUGARS 6G | PROTEIN 3G | VITAMIN A 220% | VITAMIN C 20% | CALCIUM 6% | IRON 6%

# Chilled Summer Tomato Soup with Vegetables & Basil Cream

*Have you ever had a bumper crop of garden-fresh tomatoes? Or, does your local farm stand sell heirloom varieties of the fruit in season? This is the place to celebrate those glorious summer tomatoes. While this soup shares some of the same ingredients as Avocado Guacamole Soup (page 22), the cool purée of ripe, juicy tomatoes along with aromatic vegetables, a pinch of saffron, and a splash of Pastis, will transport you to the south of France.*

*Serve the soup cool, not cold, to savor the full flavor. It's easily multiplied and oh so refreshing on a sultry summer night. Along with the basil-and-lemon-scented cream topping, a simple salsa of finely diced cucumber, avocado, and red onion is stirred in before serving. If you prefer, omit the cream and simply stir in the basil. Serve with Herbed Tortilla Crisps.*

SERVES 4

2 teaspoons extra-virgin olive oil

1 small rib celery, trimmed and sliced

1 small onion, peeled and sliced

1 small leek, white part only, rinsed to remove grit, sliced

1 medium red bell pepper, seeds and membranes removed, sliced

½ small fennel bulb, trimmed and sliced

8 large cloves garlic, split

4 pounds large, ripe heirloom or beefsteak tomatoes, cored and coarsely chopped

1 bouquet garni of 4 sprigs flat-leaf parsley, 2 sprigs thyme, 2 large sprigs basil, tied with string

1 cup water

¼ teaspoon saffron threads

¼ cup Pastis or other anise-flavored liqueur (optional)

Salt and freshly ground white pepper

¼ cup red onion cut into ⅛-inch dice

¼ cup English cucumber, peeled, seeded, and cut into ⅛-inch dice

¼ cup ripe avocado, cut into ⅛-inch dice

1 teaspoon fresh lemon juice

⅓ cup sour cream or plain soy yogurt

2 tablespoons heavy cream, light cream, or soy milk

Finely grated zest of ½ lemon

10 large fresh basil leaves

Herbed Tortilla Crisps (page 141) (optional)

1. Heat the olive oil in a large heavy, nonreactive casserole over medium–low heat. Stir in the celery, onion, leek, bell pepper, fennel, and garlic. Cover and sweat until the vegetables are tender, about 10 minutes.

2. Add the tomatoes, bouquet garni, water, and saffron, and bring to a boil. Partially cover and cook until the tomatoes are completely tender, about 15

minutes. Remove and discard the herbs. Stir in the Pastis and season to taste with salt and pepper. Let the soup cool over a bowl of ice. If you are in a hurry, omit this step. However, cooling helps the tomatoes to retain their bright red color.

3. Transfer the soup to a blender and purée until smooth, then pass it through a fine strainer, pressing to extract as much liquid as possible.

4. Combine the red onion, cucumber, and avocado in a small bowl. Add the lemon juice and a pinch of salt. Blend the sour cream and light cream in a small bowl. Chop the basil and stir it into the cream along with the lemon zest and a pinch of salt. Stir the diced vegetables into the soup. Ladle the soup into bowls, add a dollop of cream, and serve at room temperature along with Herbed Tortilla Crisps.

## NUTRITIONAL INFORMATION

CALORIES 270 | CALORIES FROM FAT 90 | TOTAL FAT 10G | SATURATED FAT 4G
CHOLESTEROL 10MG | TOTAL CARBOHYDRATE 38G | DIETARY FIBER 8G
SUGARS 19G | PROTEIN 6G | VITAMIN A 70% | VITAMIN C 190% | CALCIUM 10% | IRON 15%

# Mighty Minestrone

*This is one of my favorite soups and one-dish comfort meals. I serve it to people of all ages—from the most finicky eaters to those with very discriminating palates. Everyone seems to love it. My own secret for adding extra "oomph" or body to the soup is stirring in a can of puréed white beans. The cornucopia of fresh vegetables is only my suggestion. If you love pasta in minestrone, cook it separately and then add it close to the time when you'll serve it. You'll probably want to omit the potatoes in that case.*

SERVES AT LEAST 12

1 large rib celery, trimmed

1 medium–large onion, peeled

3 medium carrots, peeled

2 large cloves garlic, crushed

1 tablespoon olive oil

6–7 cups stock (I prefer half chicken and half beef, but you can also use vegetable stock)

2 medium potatoes, peeled and cut into ½-inch dice (optional, if using pasta)

12 ounces green cabbage, cored and shredded

4 ounces white mushrooms, trimmed, wiped, and sliced

4 ounces tender green beans, tips removed and cut into 1-inch pieces

1 medium zucchini, sliced

1 cup drained imported canned tomatoes, coarsely chopped (see sidebar)

2 tablespoons tomato paste

1 teaspoon dried oregano

1 (15-ounce) can cannellini beans, not drained, puréed

1½ cups cooked dried kidney or garbanzo beans or 1 (15-ounce) can kidney or garbanzo beans, rinsed and drained

½ cup chopped flat-leaf parsley (see sidebar)

Salt and freshly ground black pepper

Freshly grated imported Parmesan cheese or soy cheese

1. Finely chop the celery, onion, and carrots either by hand or in a food processor. If using a processor, pulse the vegetables so you don't over-chop them.

2. Heat the oil in a large heavy pot over medium–high heat. Stir in the vegetables and sauté until softened, about 5 minutes, stirring occasionally. Add the garlic, cook for 30 seconds, then 6 cups of stock, the potatoes, if using, and cabbage. Cover and bring the liquid to a gentle boil. Cook for 8 minutes, then add all remaining ingredients except the Parmesan cheese, and simmer for 20 minutes. Add the remaining stock or tomato juice, if needed. Add cooked pasta at this point, if using, and cook until heated through. Serve steaming hot with a generous sprinkling of cheese.

＊ Save That Juice!
When using canned tomatoes that you first strain, save the juice. If your soup is too thick, you can add the tomato juice along with additional stock, or use the juice in another dish or sauce.

＊ Flat-Leaf versus Curly Parsley
When cooking with parsley, I prefer the flat-leaf (aka Italian) variety because it has more flavor. For garnishing a platter, curly parsley is more attractive.

CALORIES 160 | CALORIES FROM FAT 25 | TOTAL FAT 2.5G | SATURATED FAT 0G

CHOLESTEROL 0MG | TOTAL CARBOHYDRATE 27G | DIETARY FIBER 7G

SUGARS 5G | PROTEIN 9G | VITAMIN A 80% | VITAMIN C 40% | CALCIUM 6% | IRON 20%

# Sopa de Legumbres—Minestrone New Mexico Style

LOW CARB
SMART FAT
LOW CALORIE
VEGETARIAN OR VEGAN

*This hearty vegetable soup uses ingredients native to the Americas. Corn, tomatoes, jicama, and pumpkin add texture and flavor to this spicy soup. Although the list of ingredients looks lengthy, the preparation is very quick and, once made, it gets better as it sits. Add or subtract them according to your personal taste. Use smoky ancho chili powder if you like a "kick."*

SERVES 6–8

2 tablespoons olive oil

2 cups peeled and sliced onions

2 cups shredded white cabbage

1 cup trimmed and sliced celery

½ cup peeled and diced carrots

2 cloves garlic, crushed

4 cups vegetable or chicken stock

1 cup peeled and diced jicama

1 medium red bell pepper, seeds and membranes removed, and diced

1 cup frozen small lima beans

1 cup fresh, frozen, or canned corn kernels

1 cup canned pumpkin purée

2 tablespoons tomato paste

2 teaspoons ground cumin

1 teaspoon ancho or mild chili powder, according to taste

1 teaspoon dried oregano

½ cup chopped cilantro or flat-leaf parsley

Salt and freshly ground black pepper

1 cup sour cream, to garnish (optional)

Chili-Crusted Pumpkin Seeds (page 138), to garnish

1. Heat the oil in a large pot over medium–high heat. When hot, stir in the onions, cabbage, celery, and carrots, and sauté until the carrots are almost tender, 5–6 minutes, stirring occasionally. Add the garlic, cook 30 seconds, and then blend in all the remaining ingredients. Bring the liquid to a boil, then cover, and reduce the heat so the soup is just simmering. Cook for 10–12 minutes.

2. Stir in the cilantro and season to taste with salt and pepper.

3. Ladle the soup into large bowls. Add a generous dollop of sour cream and some Chili-Crusted Pumpkin Seeds before serving.

## NUTRITIONAL INFORMATION

CALORIES 190 | CALORIES FROM FAT 90 | TOTAL FAT 10G | SATURATED FAT 3.5G
CHOLESTEROL 10MG | TOTAL CARBOHYDRATE 22G | DIETARY FIBER 6G
SUGARS 5G | PROTEIN 5G | VITAMIN A 190% | VITAMIN C 50% | CALCIUM 8% | IRON 10%

When the waitress in a New York City restaurant brought the
Englishman the soup du jour, he was rather dismayed.

"Good heavens," he said. "What's this?"

"Why, it's bean soup," she answered.

"I don't care what it's been," he replied. "What is it now?"

—An Old Joke

# bean & grain soups

# White Bean & Roasted Garlic Soup

*This reminds me of a rustic soup one might eat in Tuscany where white beans (cannellini) are served in almost every guise. Puréed roasted garlic, rosemary, and prosciutto add heady tastes to complement the mild beans. I like to serve this soup with Rosemary-Parmesan Crostini.*

SERVES 6

½ cup whole, peeled garlic cloves

1 tablespoon olive oil

4½ cups dried and cooked cannellini (white beans) or 3 (15-ounce) cans cannellini, rinsed and drained

2–2½ cups chicken or vegetable stock

¾ cup peeled, seeded, and diced plum tomatoes or drained imported canned tomatoes

2 (4–5-inch) sprigs rosemary

2 ounces prosciutto or smoked ham, or vegetarian bacon, finely chopped

Salt and plenty of freshly ground black pepper

Rosemary-Parmesan Crostini (page 137) (optional)

Fruity extra-virgin olive oil

1. Combine the garlic and olive oil in a small saucepan. Partially cover and cook over medium-low heat until the garlic is very soft and golden colored, about 30 minutes, stirring occasionally. Add the garlic and oil along with 3 cups of the beans to the bowl of a food processor and purée until smooth.

2. Return the purée to a large saucepan. Add 2 cups of stock, the remaining beans, tomatoes, rosemary sprigs, and prosciutto. Bring the mixture to a boil, reduce the heat, and simmer for 30 minutes, adding more stock if the soup is too thick. Remove the rosemary sprigs, season to taste with salt and pepper, and keep warm over low heat.

3. Prepare the crostini, if using. Serve in bowls with a final drizzle of olive oil and a couple of crostini.

## NUTRITIONAL INFORMATION

CALORIES 250 | CALORIES FROM FAT 40 | TOTAL FAT 4.5G | SATURATED FAT 0.5G
CHOLESTEROL 5MG | TOTAL CARBOHYDRATE 38G | DIETARY FIBER 9G
SUGARS 4G | PROTEIN 16G | VITAMIN A 4% | VITAMIN C 15% | CALCIUM 8% | IRON 25%

# Pumpkin Black Bean Soup

*Far from mundane black bean soup, this Caribbean-inspired version boasts the complex marriage of pumpkin, beans, tomatoes, ham, and sherry wine. Friends request it and when served, they often take second or third helpings. I top it with a shower of spicy pumpkin seeds instead of croutons. For a festive soup tureen, present the soup in a pumpkin shell. Serve with a little glass of sherry. It's magical.*

LOW CARB

SMART FAT

LOW CALORIE

VEGETARIAN OR VEGAN

SERVES 6

3 cups dried and cooked black beans or 2 (15-ounce) cans black beans, drained

1 cup drained diced canned tomatoes

1 cup canned or puréed fresh pumpkin

6 ounces boiled ham, cut into ⅛ -inch cubes (optional)

2½–3 cups beef, chicken, or vegetable stock

2 tablespoons olive oil

1½ cups finely chopped onions

3 large cloves garlic, minced

1 tablespoon ground cumin

Salt (2–3 teaspoons) and freshly ground black pepper

3–4 tablespoons sherry vinegar

½–¾ cup medium sherry or white grape juice

Sour cream or plain soy yogurt, to garnish (optional)

Chili-Crusted Pumpkin Seeds (page 138), to garnish (optional)

1. Combine the beans and tomatoes in a food processor and pulse until the beans have started to smooth out but are still somewhat chunky. Scrape into a saucepan. Stir in the pumpkin, ham, and 2 ½ cups of stock.

2. Heat the olive oil in a large skillet over medium heat. Add the onions and sauté until lightly colored, 8–10 minutes. Add the garlic and cook for 30 seconds more. Stir in the cumin, then add to the bean mixture. Stir in the salt, pepper, and vinegar.

3. Bring the soup to a boil, then reduce the heat, and simmer for 15–20 minutes. Stir in ½ cup of sherry and taste to adjust the seasonings. Add the remaining stock and sherry, as needed, and reheat, if needed. Serve in large bowls and top with sour cream or yogurt and Chili-Crusted Pumpkin Seeds, if desired.

## NUTRITIONAL INFORMATION

CALORIES 180 | CALORIES FROM FAT 50 | TOTAL FAT 6G | SATURATED FAT 1G

CHOLESTEROL 10MG | TOTAL CARBOHYDRATE 18G | DIETARY FIBER 5G

SUGARS 4G | PROTEIN 8G | VITAMIN A 140% | VITAMIN C 10% | CALCIUM 6% | IRON 15%

✳ A Festive Pumpkin Tureen

For an attractive pumpkin tureen, choose a large, handsome but rather squat pumpkin. Wash it with warm, soapy water and dry well.

Using a sharp paring knife, cut off the top quarter in a zigzag pattern. Scoop out the strings and seeds with a large metal spoon. If desired, clean and reserve the seeds for Chili-Crusted Pumpkin Seeds. Brush the entire pumpkin, inside and out, with a little vegetable oil.

Oil a heavy baking sheet (or use two sheets, one on top of the other, to support the pumpkin's weight). Preheat the oven to 325°F. Bake the pumpkin and lid on the sheet until it is warmed through and slightly softened, but still holding its shape. Begin checking after about 1 hour. Don't let it overcook and become completely soft or the tureen won't hold the soup.

Ladle the hot soup into the pumpkin and serve, using the lid as a cover, if desired.

After the soup is served and the tureen is empty, scraped out and freeze the cooked pumpkin for the next time you make this soup.

# Split Green Pea Soup

*For years, split pea soup with ham or kielbasa was a family favorite. When my son Ben became a vegetarian, I devised this version using parsnips instead of meat and vegetable stock for chicken stock.*

SERVES 6–8

2 medium–large carrots, peeled and trimmed

2 medium ribs celery, trimmed

1 large onion, peeled

2 medium–large parsnips, peeled and trimmed

2 tablespoons vegetable oil

1 pound green split peas

4 cups chicken or vegetable stock

3–4 cups water

1 ham bone or 12 ounces spicy Spanish lamb sausages, cooked (optional)

1 teaspoon dried thyme leaves

1 bay leaf

Salt and freshly ground black pepper

Croutons or toasted thin slices of a baguette (optional)

1. Finely chop the carrots, celery, onion, and parsnips either by hand or in a food processor. If using a processor, pulse the vegetables so you don't over-chop them.

2. Heat the oil in a large, heavy pot over medium–high heat. Stir in the vegetables, reduce the heat to medium, and sauté until softened, 10–12 minutes, stirring occasionally.

3. Add the split peas, stock, 3 cups of the water, the ham bone, if using (see sidebar), thyme, bay leaf, and salt and pepper to taste. Bring the mixture to a boil, cover, and reduce the heat so the liquid is simmering. Cook until the peas are very tender, about 1–1¼ hours.

4. Remove the bay leaf. Transfer the mixture to a food processor and pulse until chunky–smooth. Return to the pot. The soup should be rather thick, but stir in some of the remaining water if needed. Add the sausages, if using, and heat until hot, then serve topped with croutons or toasts, if desired.

* **Meaty Pea Soup**
  A ham bone may be added for the traditional version. Or for smaller households, boil ham hocks for the soup stock, then add the cooked meat to the soup. I actually prefer to add cooked spicy Moroccan lamb sausages, or merguez. They infuse the soup with tantalizing, exotic flavors. But any relatively flavorful sausage may be substituted.

## NUTRITIONAL INFORMATION

CALORIES 350 | CALORIES FROM FAT 60 | TOTAL FAT 7G | SATURATED FAT 1G

CHOLESTEROL 0MG | TOTAL CARBOHYDRATE 55G | DIETARY FIBER 22G

SUGARS 8G | PROTEIN 20G | VITAMIN A 90% | VITAMIN C 15% | CALCIUM 8% | IRON 20%

# Better than Grandma's Mushroom Barley Soup

LOW CARB
LOW CALORIE
VEGETARIAN OR VEGAN

*For generations, mushroom-barley soup has brought warmth and comfort to millions on cold winter days. Here's an updated version.*

½ cup medium barley, picked over

1½ ounces dried sliced porcini or other wild mushrooms

4 tablespoons vegetable oil

½ pound each parsnips, carrots, and onions, finely chopped

1 large clove garlic, minced

8 ounces white mushrooms, wiped, trimmed, and finely chopped

3 cups beef, chicken, or vegetable stock

1½ teaspoons fresh thyme leaves or ½ tsp dried thyme leaves

1 bay leaf

Salt and freshly ground black pepper

1 cup whole milk or soy milk

2–3 tablespoons fresh lemon juice

SERVES 6–8

1. Bring 2 cups of water to a boil in a small saucepan. Add the barley, lower the heat, and cook until tender, about 25 minutes. Drain and set aside.

2. Cover the porcini with 1¼ cups of hot water and soak until softened. Squeeze dry and discard any hard bits. Pour the liquid through a fine strainer and reserve. You should have about 1 cup of liquid.

3. Meanwhile, heat the oil in a large heavy casserole over medium heat. Add the parsnips, carrots, and onions, cover, and sweat over medium–low heat until tender, about 10 minutes, stirring occasionally. Add the garlic, cook for 1 minute, then stir in the fresh mushrooms and cook about 3 minutes.

4. Add the porcini, the reserved soaking liquid, the stock, thyme, and bay leaf. Partially cover and simmer for 10 minutes. Remove the bay leaf and, if desired, transfer the soup to a food processor and pulse until chunky-smooth.

5. Return the soup to the pot, stir in the barley, and bring to a boil. Season to taste with salt and pepper. Stir in the milk and, if needed, more stock, and the lemon juice. Taste to adjust the seasonings, heat until hot, and serve.

## NUTRITIONAL INFORMATION

CALORIES 190 | CALORIES FROM FAT 80 | TOTAL FAT 9G | SATURATED FAT 1.5G

CHOLESTEROL <5MG | TOTAL CARBOHYDRATE 24G | DIETARY FIBER 5G

SUGARS 5G | PROTEIN 5G | VITAMIN A 160% | VITAMIN C 20% | CALCIUM 6% | IRON 8%

# Rosemary-Scented Chickpea & Bay Scallop Soup

*Show off the finest bay scallops you can buy in this rosemary-scented garbanzo bean soup. The scallops, gently poached and stirred in at the last minute, are succulent, sweet morsels. The dollop of rosemary cream is a luxurious revelation. Rosemary is bruised and then steeped in heated cream. ("Bruising" an aromatic herb or garlic means to slightly crush or mash it in order to release its flavor.)*

*I originally tasted this exciting pairing of flavors in a dish of scallops poached in a cup of olive oil with garbanzos and rosemary whipped cream. It was prepared by Chef Tom Colicchio, today one of New York's brightest stars. Brilliant though that dish was, I eliminated most of the oil and puréed it into luscious soup. Do take time to soak dried garbanzos. In this soup, you can really appreciate the difference in the texture and taste the difference between them and canned beans.*

**SERVES 4**

1 sprig fresh rosemary

½ cup heavy cream

2 teaspoons + 1 tablespoon extra-virgin olive oil

1 small carrot, scraped and cut into 2-inch pieces

1 small rib celery, trimmed and cut into 2-inch pieces

1 small onion, peeled and cut in half

½ cup dried chickpeas, soaked either overnight or by the quick method (see sidebar)

3 cups chicken stock

1 bay leaf

1 pound bay scallops, blotted dry

2 tablespoons finely diced peeled and seeded tomato

¼ teaspoon minced fresh rosemary leaves

Salt and freshly ground black pepper

1. Bruise the rosemary, then combine it with the cream in a small saucepan. Heat until just below the boiling point. Turn off the heat and let the rosemary steep for 30 minutes. Remove the sprig and refrigerate the cream in a small bowl until cold.

2. Heat 2 teaspoons of olive oil in a medium saucepan over medium–high heat. When hot, add the carrot, celery, and onion, cover pan, lower the heat, and sweat vegetables until wilted, 10–15 minutes. Add the chickpeas, 1½

cups of the stock, and the bay leaf. Simmer until the chickpeas are completely soft, 45–50 minutes. Discard the vegetables and the bay leaf.

3. Transfer the chickpeas and stock to a food processor and pulse until only slightly chunky. Return the mixture to the pan and add the remaining stock. Stir in the tomato and rosemary and bring the soup to a simmer.

4. Beat the reserved cream into soft peaks.

5. Heat the remaining tablespoon of olive oil in a saucepan. Add the scallops and gently sauté until barely cooked through, 1–1½ minutes, then scrape into the soup. Season to taste with salt and pepper, ladle the soup into wide, flat bowls, add a generous dollop of rosemary cream, and serve.

## NUTRITIONAL INFORMATION

CALORIES 340 | CALORIES FROM FAT 210 | TOTAL FAT 23G | SATURATED FAT 8G
CHOLESTEROL 75MG | TOTAL CARBOHYDRATE 12G | DIETARY FIBER 2G
SUGARS 3G | PROTEIN 22G | VITAMIN A 80% | VITAMIN C 10% | CALCIUM 6% | IRON 4%

✴ Soaking Dried Beans

There are two methods of soaking dried chickpeas (garbanzo beans) and other beans. The traditional method involves soaking them overnight in a large pot of water, then discarding the water before bringing them to a boil in a large pot of water and cooking them until they are tender, about one hour.

For the second or "quick" method, put the beans in a pot with enough cold water to cover. Cover the pot and bring the water to a boil. Cook for 2 minutes, turn off the heat and let them stand for 1 hour before the second cooking. Both methods work well. However, very old beans seem to require more cooking to become tender.

You should not, however, add salt to beans as you cook them because it toughens them. Season them after they are already thoroughly cooked.

# Pasta & Chickpea Soup

*Nancy Radke has been a passionate spokesperson for Parmigiano-Reggiano for many years. The real Italian version of this cheese is believed by many to be the finest hard grating cheese for its nutty, full flavor, and I agree. Nancy shared her version of this much-loved hearty Italian soup with me. Like many economical Italian housewives, she adds the cheese rind to the bubbling soup to impart extra flavor. That softened rind is so yummy to eat, too! (Ask a friendly cheese retailer to save it when he trims a whole wheel of cheese.)*

SERVES 6–8

2 ounces thinly sliced prosciutto or ham

1 small red onion, peeled

1 medium carrot, scraped and trimmed

1 medium rib celery, trimmed

1 large clove garlic

1½ teaspoons fresh rosemary leaves or ½ teaspoon dried rosemary leaves

3 tablespoons olive oil

1 (28-ounce) can finest-quality crushed plum tomatoes

4 cups chicken stock

2 (15-ounce) cans chickpeas, rinsed and drained or 3 cups cooked chickpeas (see sidebar on page 69)

1 tablespoon tomato paste

1 bay leaf

1 (4-inch) square of Parmigiano-Reggiano rind (optional)

Salt and freshly ground black pepper

1 cup small pasta tubes (ditali)

Freshly grated Parmigiano-Reggiano cheese

1. Finely chop the prosciutto, red onion, carrot, celery, and garlic either by hand or in a food processor. If using a processor, pulse the vegetables so you don't over-chop them. Heat the oil in a large heavy pot over medium heat. When hot, stir in the vegetable mixture and sauté until softened, about 8 minutes.

2. Add all remaining ingredients through the Parmigiano-Reggiano rind. Bring the soup to a gentle simmer, partially cover, and cook for 30 minutes, stirring occasionally. Remove the softened Parmigiano-Reggiano rind, cut it into ¼-inch cubes, and return to the soup. Season to taste with salt and plenty of black pepper. If it is too thick, add additional stock or water. (The soup may be made ahead to this point.)

3. Before serving, add the pasta to simmering soup. When it is al dente, ladle the soup into bowls and sprinkle generously with cheese.

CALORIES 230 | CALORIES FROM FAT 80 | TOTAL FAT 9G | SATURATED FAT 1.5G
CHOLESTEROL 5MG | TOTAL CARBOHYDRATE 29G | DIETARY FIBER 5G
SUGARS 2G | PROTEIN 9G | VITAMIN A 70% | VITAMIN C 20% | CALCIUM 10% | IRON 15%

# Ginger & Lentil Soup

*My friend Fern Berman, a public relations powerhouse in New York City, says this soup gets her through every winter crisis. And why not? We all know about chicken soup's benefits. Well, ginger and garlic are also reputed to have healthful properties, and this soup has plenty of both. Vary the quantity of ingredients according to your own taste. If you want to make this humble soup heartier, add cooked dark meat chicken or duck, or diced tofu.*

SERVES 8

2 tablespoons extra-virgin olive oil

1 large onion, peeled and chopped

5–6 cloves garlic, chopped

3–4 tablespoons grated fresh gingerroot

4 medium carrots, peeled and diced

3¾ cups water

1 pound dried lentils, rinsed and picked over for foreign particles

6 cups chicken or vegetable stock

Salt and freshly ground black pepper to taste

2–3 teaspoons of balsamic vinegar or to taste

1. Heat the olive oil in a large, heavy pot over medium heat. Add the onion, garlic, and ginger and sauté until transparent, about 6 minutes. Add ¾ cup water and the diced carrots and simmer a minute. Stir in the lentils, then add the stock and remaining 3 cups of water. Partly cover and simmer over low heat until the lentils are cooked and the soup has the consistency of porridge, about 40 minutes, stirring often.

2. Remove from the heat, stir in salt, pepper, and balsamic vinegar to taste. Ladle into bowls and serve.

## NUTRITIONAL INFORMATION

CALORIES 260 | CALORIES FROM FAT 0.5 | TOTAL FAT 5G | SATURATED FAT 0.5G

CHOLESTEROL 0MG | TOTAL CARBOHYDRATE 38G | DIETARY FIBER 18G

SUGARS 6G | PROTEIN 17G | VITAMIN A 130% | VITAMIN C 10% | CALCIUM 4% | IRON 30%

# Red Lentil Apricot Soup

*Dried apricots impart a subtle but delightful sweetness to this nicely spiced red lentil soup. Hannah Duckworth, a friend of my daughter, sent this recipe from her mom, Mo, of Birch Vale, Derbyshire, England.*

1 tablespoon olive oil

1 large onion, peeled and chopped

3 cloves garlic, finely chopped

1 teaspoon ground cumin

1 teaspoon ground coriander seeds

1 teaspoon ground fennel seeds

3 medium carrots, peeled and diced

½ cup chopped dried apricots

1½ cups red lentils, rinsed and picked over for foreign particles

7 cups vegetable stock

Salt and freshly ground black pepper

2 tablespoons crème fraîche or sour cream

1 tablespoon chopped fresh thyme leaves or flat-leaf parsley, to garnish

SERVES 6–8

1. Heat the oil in a large heavy casserole over medium–high heat. Add the onion and sauté until golden, about 5 minutes. Stir in the garlic, cumin, coriander, and fennel, and cook for 1 minute. Add the carrots and apricots, partially cover, and cook over low heat for 5 minutes.

2. Stir in the lentils and stock, cover, and simmer until the lentils and carrots are tender, 45 minutes to an hour, stirring occasionally.

3. Using an immersion blender, blend the soup until chunky–smooth. Or transfer it to the bowl of a food processor and pulse until it reaches the right consistency.

4. Return the soup to the pot and season to taste with salt and pepper. Reheat if necessary, then stir in the crème fraîche and herbs, ladle into bowls, and serve.

## NUTRITIONAL INFORMATION

CALORIES 190 | CALORIES FROM FAT 40 | TOTAL FAT 4G | SATURATED FAT 0.5G

CHOLESTEROL 0MG | TOTAL CARBOHYDRATE 28G | DIETARY FIBER 13G

SUGARS 5G | PROTEIN 12G | VITAMIN A 80% | VITAMIN C 8% | CALCIUM 4% | IRON 20%

# Madras Red Lentil Soup

*This is one of the most beautifully seasoned soups I have ever tasted. It comes from my friend Najmieh Batmanglij, a food historian and cook who lives in Washington, D.C. Do look for the spices she recommends. It'll be worth the effort when you taste this soup.*

SERVES 6

2½ cups red lentils, picked over for foreign particles

4 tablespoons vegetable oil or clarified butter

1 tablespoon cumin seeds

1 teaspoon each coriander, fenugreek, and mustard seeds

1 medium onion, peeled and thinly sliced

4 curry leaves, available at Indian and Asian grocery stores

2 cloves garlic, crushed

1-inch piece fresh gingerroot, peeled and grated

1 Thai bird or jalapeño chile, chopped, or ½ teaspoon cayenne pepper

2 teaspoons salt

1 teaspoon sugar or sugar substitute

½ teaspoon ground turmeric

6 cups water

2 tablespoons rice flour, dissolved in 2 cups cold water (see note)

2 cups canned diced tomatoes

2 tablespoons fresh lime juice

1 cup chopped fresh cilantro, to garnish

1. In a bowl, cover the lentils with water and agitate them with your hands, then drain. Repeat until the water is clear, then set aside.

2. Heat the oil or butter in a medium-size heavy casserole over medium heat. Add the cumin, coriander, fenugreek, and mustard seeds and cook for 10 seconds or until the seeds stop crackling (keep a lid handy to help prevent the seeds from popping out). Add the onion and curry leaves, and stir-fry until the onion is translucent, about 10 minutes. Stir in the garlic, ginger, chili pepper or cayenne, salt, sugar, and turmeric, and cook 1 minute longer.

3. Add the red lentils and water and bring to a boil. Reduce the heat, partially cover, and simmer until the lentils are tender, about 30 minutes. Discard the curry leaves. Mash the lentils with a hand-held mixer or the back of a large wooden spoon until the mixture is chunky-smooth.

4. Add the diluted rice flour, tomatoes, and lime juice, and bring the soup back to a boil. Reduce the heat, partially cover, and simmer for 15 minutes longer.

5. Before serving, taste to adjust the seasonings. Ladle the soup into bowls and garnish with cilantro.

**NOTE:** Rice flour is made from finely ground grains of white or brown rice. It has no gluten (for those with allergies) and is a good thickener for soups, stews, and sweets. It is sold in some supermarkets and health food stores. If you have an electric spice grinder, you can make your own.

### NUTRITIONAL INFORMATION

CALORIES 410 | CALORIES FROM FAT 100 | TOTAL FAT 11G | SATURATED FAT 1.5G
CHOLESTEROL 0MG | TOTAL CARBOHYDRATE 56G | DIETARY FIBER 26G
SUGARS 9G | PROTEIN 25G | VITAMIN A 30% | VITAMIN C 45% | CALCIUM 8% | IRON 50%

# Winter Chestnut Soup with Duck Confit

*At first glance, this velvety-smooth soup might appear mild-mannered and bland. Don't be fooled. The jalapeño pepper, warm blend of spices, and caramelized garlic add layers of flavor that impart a faraway glamour to the subtle sweetness of the chestnuts and fennel. As for all those 20 garlic cloves, don't be afraid—cooking tames their bite and makes them deliciously mild.*

SERVES 4

20 large cloves garlic, peeled

2 tablespoons olive oil

8 ounces fresh chestnuts, roasted and peeled, or canned/bottled peeled, unsweetened chestnuts, drained

1 medium onion, peeled and sliced

1 small fennel bulb, fronds trimmed and discarded, sliced

1 jalapeño pepper, seeded, deveined and finely chopped

1 teaspoon coriander

½ teaspoon each cardamom, cinnamon, coriander, cumin, ginger, and mace

½ cup dry white wine

1 bay leaf

2 cups chicken or vegetable stock

½ cup heavy cream

Salt and freshly ground white pepper

¼ cup medium Madeira or apple juice

8 ounces duck confit, cut into ¼-inch dice, available from specialty butchers or D'Artagnan (1.800.327.8246) or 8 ounces vegetarian sausage

2 tablespoons chopped flat-leaf parsley

1. Combine the garlic cloves and 1 tablespoon of oil in a small heavy pan, partially cover, and cook over low heat until the garlic is very soft and golden color, about 25 minutes, shaking the pan occasionally. Watch that they don't burn. Set aside. (Alternatively, roast two whole heads of garlic ahead of time in the oven, perhaps while baking something else, at a moderate temperature. To do so, cut off ¼ inch from the pointed end of the heads, rub with olive oil, wrap in aluminum foil, and bake until tender, about 30-35 minutes. Let cool and squeeze out the garlic cloves.)

2. Heat the remaining tablespoon of oil in a large heavy casserole over medium–high heat. When hot, add the chestnuts, onion, fennel, jalapeño, cover and sweat over medium heat until the vegetables are tender, about 15 minutes, stirring occasionally. Add the coriander, cardamom, cinnamon, coriander, cumin, ginger, mace, and bay leaf, and cook 1 minute more.

3. Pour in the white wine, bring the liquid to a boil, and reduce by half. Stir in the stock, then transfer the mixture to the jar of an electric blender along with the softened garlic, and purée in batches until smooth.

4. Pour the soup through a fine strainer and return it to the pan. Stir in the cream and Madeira, season with salt and pepper to taste, and bring the soup to a boil. Reduce the heat and keep warm.

5. Sauté the diced duck confit or sausage in a nonstick pan over high heat until crisp. Remove with a slotted spoon, and divide it among four warm soup bowls. Ladle the soup over the confit or sausage, sprinkle with parsley, and serve.

* Duck Soup (A Famous Persian Story)

A relative came to see Mulla Nasruddin from the country, and brought a duck. Mulla was grateful and had the bird cooked, and shared it with his guest.

Presently, another visitor arrived. He was a friend, as he said, "of the man who gave you the duck." Mulla fed him as well.

This happened several times. Mulla's home had become like a restaurant for out-of-town visitors. Everyone was a more and more distantly removed friend of the original donor of the duck.

Finally, Mulla was exasperated. One day there was a knock at the door, and a stranger appeared. "I am the friend of the friend of the friend of the man who brought you the duck from the country," he said.

"Come in," said Mulla Nasruddin.

They seated themselves at the table, and Nasruddin asked his wife to bring the soup.

When the guest tasted it, it seemed to be nothing more than warm water.

"What sort of soup is this?"" he asked Mulla.

"That," said Mulla, "is the soup of the soup of the soup of the duck."

NUTRITIONAL INFORMATION

CALORIES 480 | CALORIES FROM FAT 230 | TOTAL FAT 26G | SATURATED FAT 10G
CHOLESTEROL 90MG | TOTAL CARBOHYDRATE 38G | DIETARY FIBER 3G
SUGARS 2G | PROTEIN 17G | VITAMIN A 15% | VITAMIN C 70% | CALCIUM 10% | IRON 20%

# Tortellini Soup

SMART FAT
LOW CALORIE
VEGETARIAN

*With its last-minute basil-Parmesan topping, and drizzle of fragrant extra-virgin olive oil, this simple soup really tastes homemade. I make the broth-greens mixture ahead of time and then add the pasta and simmer them just before I'm ready to eat. Use the finest-quality prepared ingredients and you'll taste the difference. I like tortellini filled with ricotta, Parmesan cheese, and basil.*

2 teaspoons extra-virgin olive oil + extra for topping

1 small onion, peeled and chopped

2 large cloves garlic, minced

4 ounces fresh kale or other leafy greens, coarse ribs removed and thinly shredded

7 cups chicken or vegetable stock

1 (9-ounce) package frozen basil-Parmesan tortellini or other flavors (including vegetarian fillings)

Basil-Parmesan Topping (recipe follows)

Salt and freshly ground black pepper

SERVES 6–8

1. Heat the oil in a large, heavy pot over medium heat. When hot, add onion and garlic and sauté until limp, 3–4 minutes. Add the kale and stock, and bring the liquid to a boil. Stir in the tortellini, reduce the heat, and gently boil until the tortellini are tender, about 8 minutes. Don't overcook.

2. Meanwhile, prepare the Basil-Parmesan Topping.

3. Season the soup to taste with salt and pepper. Ladle into large soup bowls, drizzle on some olive oil, generously sprinkle with a tablespoon or two of the topping and serve.

## Basil-Parmesan Topping

¾ cup freshly-grated imported Parmesan cheese

¼ cup finely chopped fresh basil leaves

Coarsely ground black pepper to taste

Blend the Parmesan, basil, and pepper in a small bowl.

### NUTRITIONAL INFORMATION WITH TOPPING

CALORIES 210 | CALORIES FROM FAT 60 | TOTAL FAT 6G | SATURATED FAT 2G

CHOLESTEROL 5MG | TOTAL CARBOHYDRATE 28G | DIETARY FIBER 1G

SUGARS 0G | PROTEIN 10G | VITAMIN A 25% | VITAMIN C 25% | CALCIUM 15% | IRON 10%

*Soup and fish explain half the emotions of human life.*

—Sydney Smith

# fish soups

# Providence-Style Clam Chowder

*Which is better, Boston or New York–style clam chowder? This creamy fish soup with tomatoes sits in between. It may be made ahead of time, but don't freeze it. As a shortcut, use frozen or canned clams and purchased broth.*

SERVES 8–10

24 chowder clams, scrubbed, or about 2 cups frozen or canned clams

3 cups water or 6 cups clam broth, if using frozen or canned clams

2 ounces salt pork, cut into ¼ -inch cubes (or substitute 1 tablespoon olive oil)

3 medium carrots, peeled and finely chopped

1 large onion, peeled and finely chopped

1 large green bell pepper, seeds and membranes removed, finely chopped

1 large clove garlic, minced

Salt and freshly ground black pepper

1 bay leaf

1 teaspoon dried thyme leaves, crushed

1 large red potato, peeled and diced (about 2 cups)

1 cup heavy or light cream

2 cups drained finely diced canned Italian tomatoes

2 tablespoons chopped flat-leaf parsley

1. Put the clams in a large pot, add water, cover with a tight-fitting lid, and gently boil until the clams open, about 10–12 minutes. Remove the clam meat, coarsely chop, cover, and set aside. Discard the shells. Strain the liquid through a double thickness of dampened paper towels or cheesecloth and set aside. You should have about 6 cups of liquid. If using canned or frozen clams, chop the clams and add them and the clam broth in Step 3.

2. Rinse and dry the pot. Add the salt pork, if using, and sauté it over medium heat until lightly colored, about 3 minutes, stirring constantly. Stir in the carrots, onion, green pepper, and garlic, cover, and sweat over medium–low heat until the vegetables are just tender, about 8–10 minutes. Season to taste with salt and pepper.

3. Add the reserved clam broth, bay leaf, thyme, potatoes, and chopped clams, and simmer for 40 minutes.

4. Stir in the cream, tomatoes, and parsley, and simmer for another 10 minutes. Taste for seasonings, ladle into bowls, and serve.

## NUTRITIONAL INFORMATION

CALORIES 230 | CALORIES FROM FAT 100 | TOTAL FAT 11G | SATURATED FAT 6G

CHOLESTEROL 85MG | TOTAL CARBOHYDRATE 12G | DIETARY FIBER 2G

SUGARS 3G | PROTEIN 21G | VITAMIN A 110% | VITAMIN C 70% | CALCIUM 10% | IRON 110%

# Scallop & Vegetable Chowder

*This steamy chowder is far more flavorful than it looks. Fragrant winter vegetables are simmered in milk, then finely chopped and combined with scallops. Add the scallops at the last minute to keep them at their best. This is a great place to use up leftover broccoli stems, since they are hardly visible.*

*Because of the delicate nature of the scallops, once the soup is cooked, they should be eaten at that time rather than reheated. However, you can either divide the recipe in half or make the entire recipe without the scallops. Heat whatever amount of the soup you'd like and add the appropriate amount of scallops. The soup will keep for 3–4 days in the refrigerator. It's best not to freeze it.*

1 tablespoon unsalted butter or olive oil

1 medium onion, peeled and thinly sliced

1 medium potato, peeled and cut into ½-inch cubes

5 ounces broccoli, coarsely chopped

5 ounces cauliflower, coarsely chopped

3 small carrots, peeled and coarsely chopped

2 cups milk

1 cup clam broth

2–3 tablespoons snipped fresh dill or 2 teaspoons dried dill

1 cup light cream

1 pound bay scallops or chopped sea scallops

Salt and freshly ground black pepper

SERVES 6–8

1. Heat the butter or oil in a large heavy saucepan over medium–high heat. Add the onion and sauté until golden, about 5–6 minutes. Add the potato, broccoli, cauliflower, carrots, milk, and clam broth and gently simmer until the vegetables are tender, about 20–25 minutes.

2. Transfer the mixture to a food processor and pulse until the vegetables are chopped into tiny pieces but not totally smooth. Return the soup to the pan, stir in the dill and light cream, and heat until hot over medium heat.

3. Stir in the scallops and cook until just opaque, 1½–2 minutes. Season to taste with salt and pepper, ladle into bowls, and serve at once.

## NUTRITIONAL INFORMATION

CALORIES 210 | CALORIES FROM FAT 100 | TOTAL FAT 11G | SATURATED FAT 6G

CHOLESTEROL 50MG | TOTAL CARBOHYDRATE 13G | DIETARY FIBER 2G

SUGARS 5G | PROTEIN 14G | VITAMIN A 100% | VITAMIN C 50% | CALCIUM 15% | IRON 4%

# Corn & Shrimp Chowder

*This chowder is so soul-satisfying, no one will guess that it's also quick and easy to make. It is one of my family's favorite soups and I frequently make huge quantities of it for casual buffets. A chowder is generally a thick soup, often with fish or shellfish in it, and frequently in a milk or cream base. It derives from the French word for kettle or cauldron, chaudière.*

3 cups defrosted frozen or fresh corn kernels

2 tablespoons unsalted butter or olive oil

1 cup chopped onion

2 cups fish stock or bottled clam broth

1 cup light cream or half-and-half

2 teaspoons sugar

½ each medium green and red bell pepper, seeds and membranes removed, and finely chopped

¾ pound fresh or frozen medium shrimp, peeled, deveined, and cut into ¾-inch slices

⅓ cup chopped fresh cilantro leaves + extra leaves to garnish

Salt and freshly ground black pepper

SERVES 4–6

1. Purée 2 cups of the corn in a food processor until smooth. Set aside.

2. Heat the butter or oil in a medium-sized heavy saucepan over medium-high heat. Add the onions and sauté until wilted, 3–4 minutes. Stir in the puréed corn, fish stock, and light cream, and simmer for 2–3 minutes.

3. Stir in the remaining corn, bell peppers, shrimp, cilantro, and salt and pepper. Gently simmer until the shrimp are just cooked through. Ladle into heated bowls, garnish with the remaining cilantro leaves, and serve.

## NUTRITIONAL INFORMATION

CALORIES 260 | CALORIES FROM FAT 130 | TOTAL FAT 14G | SATURATED FAT 8G

CHOLESTEROL 125MG | TOTAL CARBOHYDRATE 22G | DIETARY FIBER 2G

SUGARS 6G | PROTEIN 16G | VITAMIN A 20% | VITAMIN C 50% | CALCIUM 8% | IRON 10%

# Tomato Bisque with Shrimp

*A luscious saffron-scented bisque to dazzle your tastebuds on festive occasions. Although this soup tastes rich, the heavy cream used in many bisques has been replaced with milk and light cream. It may be made a couple of days ahead and reheated, or served at room temperature.*

*Bisques, while similar to chowders, are creamy soups usually made with shellfish. Because of their smooth texture, they are considered more refined than chowders by some cooks.*

**SERVES 4 GENEROUSLY**

1 small onion, peeled

½ small carrot, scraped and trimmed

1 small rib celery, trimmed

2 tablespoons unsalted butter or vegetable oil

3 tablespoons unbleached all-purpose flour

4½ cups milk or soy milk

1 (28-ounce) can finest-quality crushed plum tomatoes

4 tablespoons tomato paste

Generous pinch grated nutmeg

½ teaspoon dried thyme leaves

¼ teaspoon crumbled saffron threads

1 teaspoon sugar

1 cup light cream or soy creamer

Salt and white pepper

2 tablespoons finely chopped flat-leaf parsley + 2 tablespoons minced flat-leaf parsley, to garnish

1 pound medium shrimp, peeled, deveined and chopped, or 16-ounces diced firm tofu

1. Finely chop the onion, carrot, and celery, either by hand or in a food processor. If using a processor, pulse the vegetables so you don't over-chop them.

2. Heat the butter or oil in a large heavy pot over medium–high heat. Stir in the vegetables and sauté until very soft, 4–5 minutes, stirring occasionally. Sprinkle the flour over the vegetables, stirring to coat evenly. Continue cooking for 2 minutes, scraping the pot often.

3. Whisk in 1½ cups of the milk. When smooth, gently cook for 5 minutes longer. Add the tomatoes, tomato paste, nutmeg, thyme, saffron, sugar, and simmer for 3 minutes, stirring occasionally. It will be thick.

4. Transfer the mixture to a food processor and purée until smooth. Return the purée to the pot. Add the remaining 3 cups of milk, the cream, salt and pepper to taste, parsley, and shrimp. Simmer gently until the shrimp are cooked and the soup is hot. Ladle into hot bowls, garnish with a little minced parsley, and serve at once.

CALORIES 320 | CALORIES FROM FAT 160 | TOTAL FAT 18G | SATURATED FAT 8G

CHOLESTEROL 125MG | TOTAL CARBOHYDRATE 21G | DIETARY FIBER 3G

SUGARS 14G | PROTEIN 19G | VITAMIN A 50% | VITAMIN C 10% | CALCIUM 25% | IRON 15%

# Shrimp & Sausage Gumbo

*American regional foods, such as this spicy gumbo inspired by the flavors of New Orleans, are easy to make with the availability of high-quality sausages and local seasonings, like gumbo filé. Sliced okra thickens the broth and imparts the distinctive character associated with gumbo. Many gumbos begin with a roux, but I prefer this hearty main-course soup without it.*

**SERVES 4 GENEROUSLY**

2 teaspoons vegetable oil

1 medium onion, peeled and chopped

2 large ribs celery, trimmed and chopped

1 red or green bell pepper, seeds and membranes removed, chopped

2 large cloves garlic, minced

12 ounces spicy sausages, preferably andouille or chorizo, quartered lengthwise and cut into ½-inch slices

3 cups chicken stock

2 cups canned diced plum tomatoes

1 teaspoon filé gumbo

1 teaspoon dried oregano

1 bay leaf

6 ounces okra, cut into ¼-inch slices

½ cup coarsely chopped flat-leaf parsley

¾ cup raw long-grain white or brown

12 ounces fresh or frozen medium shrimp, shelled and deveined

Salt and coarsely ground black pepper

Several dashes Tabasco sauce

2 tablespoons red wine vinegar

1. Heat the oil over medium–high heat, add the onion, celery, bell pepper, and garlic, and sauté until crisp–tender, about 4–5 minutes. Stir in the sausage and cook for another 2–3 minutes, turning frequently. Add the stock, tomatoes, filé gumbo, oregano, and bay leaf. Bring the liquid to a boil, then reduce the heat, partially cover, and simmer for 15 minutes, stirring occasionally.

2. Stir in the okra and parsley and gently boil until the okra is tender, 15–20 minutes. Meanwhile, cook the rice in a small covered pot in 1½ cups of salted boiling water until tender, about 20 minutes for white rice or 35-40 minutes for brown rice.

3. Add the shrimp to the gumbo and cook until pink, about 5 minutes. Season to taste with salt, pepper, and Tabasco sauce.

4. Turn off the heat, remove the bay leaf, stir in the vinegar, and let the soup stand for a minute. Add a mound of cooked rice in the middle of each soup bowl. Ladle the gumbo over the rice and serve piping hot.

✱ Filé Gumbo

Filé gumbo is a hallmark of Creole cooking. The dusky green seasoning, made from the dried, ground leaves of the sassafras tree, adds flavor and helps thicken the gumbo, as well.

CALORIES 400 | CALORIES FROM FAT 190 | TOTAL FAT 21G | SATURATED FAT 6G

CHOLESTEROL 130MG | TOTAL CARBOHYDRATE 30G | DIETARY FIBER 3G

SUGARS 6G | PROTEIN 23G | VITAMIN A 15% | VITAMIN C 80% | CALCIUM 10% | IRON 25%

# Leek, Potato & Mussel Soup

*Leek and potato soup is a classic in the realm of comfort soup. Add mussels to the simmering soup, and it moves from simply superb to sublime simplicity. I like the mussels served in their shells. Remove them if you prefer.*

5 large leeks, well washed

4 tablespoons unsalted butter or olive oil

1 pound baking potatoes, peeled and chopped

3 cups vegetable stock

2 cups milk

1 pound mussels, scrubbed and debearded

Salt and white pepper

2 tablespoons minced fresh chervil or flat-leaf parsley

1. Thinly slice the white and pale green parts of the leeks. You should have about 4 cups. Thinly slice about 1 cup of the remaining green parts and set aside. Heat the butter or oil in a large casserole over medium heat. Add the leeks, cover, and sweat over medium–low heat until tender, about 15 minutes, stirring occasionally. Add the potatoes and stock, and bring the liquid to a boil. Reduce the heat, cover, and simmer until potatoes are tender, about 20 minutes.

2. Transfer the mixture to the jar of an electric blender or food processor and purée until smooth. Return to pot, stir in the milk, and bring to a boil. Adjust the heat to medium, add the mussels, salt and pepper to taste, and reserved sliced leeks. Cook until the mussels open. Taste to adjust seasonings, stir in the chervil, and ladle into wide soup bowls. Discard any mussels that do not open.

\* Lovely Leek Leftovers

Home gardeners will tell you that the green parts of fresh, not too large/mature leeks, when freshly steamed, sweated, or sautéed are among the most succulent, sweet and delicious of vegetables. They are especially sweet if pulled fresh out of the garden after a few cold or frosty nights. While not appropriate for a light-colored soup like this, they'd be nice added to a lentil soup or sautéed vegetables.

## NUTRITIONAL INFORMATION

CALORIES 270 | CALORIES FROM FAT 120 | TOTAL FAT 13G | SATURATED FAT 7G
CHOLESTEROL 55MG | TOTAL CARBOHYDRATE 24G | DIETARY FIBER 2G
SUGARS 5G | PROTEIN 15G | VITAMIN A 15% | VITAMIN C 45% | CALCIUM 15% | IRON 25%

# Elegant Oyster Soup with Lemon-Parsley Pesto

*One fine October day some years ago, an acquaintance returned from the oyster festival in St. Mary's, Maryland, where she had consumed more than her quotient of the "best fried, poached, scalloped and raw oysters I ever tasted." Dropping a pint jar of the shucked creatures on my counter, she threw down the gauntlet and challenged my creativity. This sublime soup of gently poached plump, succulent oysters perfumed with lemon-parsley pesto was the result. It is just hearty enough for a light supper or, in cups, as a start to an elegant dinner.*

SERVES 4–6

1 large carrot, scraped

1 large rib celery, trimmed

1 large onion, peeled

1 large clove garlic

2 teaspoons unsalted butter or olive oil

1 teaspoon vegetable oil

½ cup dry vermouth

2 cups half-and-half

1½ cups clam broth

1 pint shucked oysters and their liquor

Salt and white pepper

Lemon-Parsley Pesto (recipe follows)

1. Finely chop the carrot, celery, onion, and remaining garlic clove either by hand or in a food processor. If using a processor, pulse the vegetables so you don't over-chop them. Heat the butter and oil in a large heavy pot over medium–high heat. When hot, add the vegetables and sauté until lightly browned, 3–4 minutes, stirring occasionally. Cover, adjust the heat to low, and sweat the vegetables until soft, 5 minutes more.

2. Pour in the vermouth, stir up any browned cooking bits, and bring the liquid to a boil for 1 minute. Stir in the half-and-half and simmer for 5 minutes. Transfer the mixture to the jar of an electric blender and purée until smooth.

3. Return the purée to the pot, stir in the clam broth, and bring the liquid to a simmer. Add the oysters and their liquor, and poach until barely done, 5–7 minutes. Season to taste with salt and white pepper. Ladle the soup into cups or bowls and serve with about 1 tablespoon of pesto in the center of each bowl (or, ½ tablespoon for a cup).

Lemon-Parsley Pesto

2 cups loosely packed flat-leaf parsley leaves

2 large cloves garlic

3 tablespoons extra-virgin olive oil

2 unsalted butter, at room temperature

½ teaspoon coarse sea salt

½ cup freshly grated Parmigiano-Reggiano cheese

Finely grated zest of 1 lemon

1–2 teaspoons fresh lemon juice

Finely chop the parsley leaves and transfer to the jar of an electric blender or food processor. Add the garlic, olive oil, butter, and salt, and purée until almost smooth. Scrape into a bowl. Stir in the cheese, lemon zest, and lemon juice to taste. Set aside.

**SOUP NUTRITIONAL INFORMATION**

CALORIES 270 | CALORIES FROM FAT 120 | TOTAL FAT 13G | SATURATED FAT 7G

CHOLESTEROL 85MG | TOTAL CARBOHYDRATE 11G | DIETARY FIBER <1G

SUGARS 2G | PROTEIN 22G | VITAMIN A 90% | VITAMIN C 35% | CALCIUM 15% | IRON 120%

**1 TABLESPOON OF LEMON-PARSLEY PESTO**

CALORIES 100 | CALORIES FROM FAT 80 | TOTAL FAT 9G | SATURATED FAT 3.5G

CHOLESTEROL 10MG | TOTAL CARBOHYDRATE 1G | DIETARY FIBER 0G

SUGARS 0G | PROTEIN 3G | VITAMIN A 20% | VITAMIN C 30% | CALCIUM 10% | IRON 6%

# Cotriade—Breton Fish Soup

*All along the coast of Brittany, fishing boats can be seen bobbing in the water. Cotriade is a local fish soup/stew that's traditionally made with the delicious, lightly salted local butter, aromatic vegetables, fragrant herbs, potatoes, and dry wine, like Muscadet. It might include sardines, mackerel, cod, and other firm-fleshed fish. Purists say it shouldn't have shellfish in it, but I first tasted this soup in Concale, where they farm tasty oysters. It's not uncommon to also find mussels, clams, and langoustines, the small, narrow European lobsters.*

*To make the low-carb version, omit the potatoes and bread.*

SERVES 4

2 tablespoons lightly salted butter or olive oil

1 small carrot, scraped and finely chopped

1 small rib celery, trimmed and finely chopped

1 small leek, white part only, well washed, finely chopped

1 small onion, peeled and finely chopped

2 cloves garlic, minced

2 cups fish stock or clam broth

1 cup dry white wine, like Muscadet

1 tablespoons tomato paste

2 large sprigs flat-leaf parsley + 2 table-spoons chopped parsley, to garnish

2 large sprigs thyme

1 bay leaf

1 large baking potato, peeled and cut into ¾-inch dice (optional)

Salt and fresh ground black pepper

1½ pounds mixed firm-fleshed fish fillets, such as cod, monkfish, and catfish, cut into large chunks

1 pound mussels, scrubbed

4 thick slices firm-textured, crusty bread, rubbed with garlic, brushed with olive oil, and lightly toasted (optional)

1. Heat the butter or oil in a large, deep casserole over medium heat. Add the carrot, celery, leek, and onion, and cook until tender, about 6–8 minutes, stirring occasionally. Add the garlic and cook 1 minute more.

2. Stir in the stock, wine, tomato paste, parsley, thyme, and bay leaf. Bring the liquid to a boil, add the potato, salt and pepper to taste, and gently boil until the potatoes are almost tender, about 15 minutes.

3. Add the fish, cover, and simmer for 10 minutes. Add the shellfish, re-cover, and cook 2 minutes longer, until they are cooked and the shells have opened. Taste to adjust seasonings.

4. Put one piece of bread, if using, in the bottom of four wide soup bowls. Using a slotted spoon, carefully transfer the fish and shellfish to the bowls, ladle on the stock, sprinkle with parsley, and serve.

**NUTRITIONAL INFORMATION**

CALORIES 340 | CALORIES FROM FAT 90 | TOTAL FAT 10G | SATURATED FAT 4.5G
CHOLESTEROL 60MG | TOTAL CARBOHYDRATE 23G | DIETARY FIBER 3G
SUGARS 4G | PROTEIN 29G | VITAMIN A 130% | VITAMIN C 35% | CALCIUM 6% | IRON 15%

# Cioppino with Rouille

*This robust fish soup/stew is said to have originated in San Francisco. It's very much like bouillabaisse, another great one-dish meal from the south of France. But this version takes a minimum of time to prepare. Monkfish, snapper, mussels, and clams are simmered in a tomato-laced broth with a hint of anise-flavored Pernod. For an eye-opening finale, garlicky red pepper mayonnaise, or rouille, is added before serving. Be sure to pass the extras at the table. Below are two versions for that topping—one uses a raw egg yolk, the other uses mayonnaise for those concerned about raw eggs. Serve this soup with crusty slices of San Francisco-style sourdough bread.*

SERVES 6
GENEROUSLY

1 tablespoon olive oil

1 medium rib celery, trimmed and coarsely chopped

1 large onion, peeled and sliced

2 medium carrots, peeled and sliced

1 large fennel bulb, ribs and base removed, sliced

2 cups bottled clam broth

¾ cup dry white wine

¼ cup Pernod

1 (28-ounce) can chopped plum tomatoes

2 tablespoons tomato paste

½ pound monkfish, cut into 1-inch cubes, or substitute lobster meat, cubed

1 pound mussels, scrubbed and debearded

12 little neck clams, washed

½ pound red snapper fillet, cut into 2-inch slices

⅓ cup chopped fresh basil leaves

¼ cup chopped flat-leaf parsley

Freshly ground black pepper to taste

Rouille (recipe follows)

1. Heat the oil in a large heavy pot over medium–high heat. When hot, but not smoking, add the celery, onion, carrots, and fennel and sauté until wilted, 5 minutes, stirring occasionally. Add the clam broth, wine, Pernod, tomatoes, and tomato paste. Bring the liquid to a boil, cover, and reduce the heat so the liquid is simmering. Cook for 10–12 minutes.

2. Meanwhile, prepare the rouille, if using.

3. Add the monkfish, mussels, and clams to the soup, re-cover the pot, and simmer for 4 minutes. Add the snapper, basil, parsley, and pepper, cover, and simmer until all the fish is cooked through, about 2 minutes more, and the mussels and clams are opened. Ladle the cioppino into heated bowls and serve with a generous tablespoon of rouille in the center of each.

## Traditional Rouille

2 large red bell peppers, roasted, peeled and seeded, blotted dry

3–4 large cloves garlic

2 egg yolks

¼ teaspoon salt or to taste

Pinch cayenne pepper

½ cup extra-virgin olive oil

1. Combine the bell peppers, garlic, egg yolks, salt, and cayenne in a food processor and process until smooth, letting the motor run for 30 seconds. Scrape down the sides. With the motor running, add the oil through the feed tube so the mixture emulsifies.

---

## Contemporary Rouille

2 large red bell peppers, roasted, peeled and seeded, blotted dry

4 cloves garlic

¾ cup mayonnaise

Pinch cayenne pepper

⅛ teaspoon salt or to taste

¼ cup extra-virgin olive oil

1. Combine the bell peppers, garlic, mayonnaise, cayenne, and salt in a food processor and process until smooth. With the motor running, add the oil through the feed tube.

### NUTRITIONAL INFORMATION FOR CIOPPINO

CALORIES 280 | CALORIES FROM FAT 60 | TOTAL FAT 7G | SATURATED FAT 1G
CHOLESTEROL 55MG | TOTAL CARBOHYDRATE 18G | DIETARY FIBER 4G
SUGARS 6G | PROTEIN 29G | VITAMIN A 100% | VITAMIN C 70% | CALCIUM 15% | IRON 50%

### 2 TABLESPOONS OF TRADITIONAL ROUILLE

CALORIES 110 | CALORIES FROM FAT 110 | TOTAL FAT 12G | SATURATED FAT 2G
CHOLESTEROL 40MG | TOTAL CARBOHYDRATE 1G | DIETARY FIBER 0G
SUGARS 0G | PROTEIN <1G | VITAMIN A 4% | VITAMIN C 25% | CALCIUM 0% | IRON 0%

### 2 TABLESPOONS OF CONTEMPORARY ROUILLE

CALORIES 140 | CALORIES FROM FAT 130 | TOTAL FAT 15G | SATURATED FAT 2G
CHOLESTEROL <5MG | TOTAL CARBOHYDRATE 1G | DIETARY FIBER 0G
SUGARS 0G | PROTEIN 0G | VITAMIN A 0% | VITAMIN C 20% | CALCIUM 0% | IRON 0%

# Mediterranean Fish Soup with Quick Aïoli

*This fragrant saffron-scented soup will transport you to the Mediterranean coast after just one spoonful. The traditional garnish, aïoli, is nice and garlicky. I take a shortcut, using a ready-made mayonnaise. Stir it into the soup before eating. Since I think it's indispensable, the nutritional analysis includes a tablespoon of aïoli. To make the low-carb version, omit the potatoes and bread.*

SERVES 6
GENEROUSLY

3½ tablespoons extra-virgin olive oil

1 teaspoon minced garlic + 1 tablespoon finely chopped garlic

½ teaspoon saffron threads, crumbled

½ cup high-quality prepared mayonnaise

Salt

1 cup chopped onion

4 cups fish stock or clam broth

1 cup dry white wine

2 tablespoons tomato paste

1 teaspoon dried thyme leaves

1 pound red-skinned potatoes, peeled and cut into ½-inch cubes

½ cup chopped flat-leaf parsley + a few leaves to garnish

2½ pounds mixed firm white-fleshed fish, such as monkfish, cod, and snapper, cut in 1-inch chunks

Freshly ground black pepper

8–12 thin slices French baguette, lightly toasted (optional)

1. Prepare the aïoli: Combine 1½ tablespoons of the olive oil, 1 tablespoon boiling water, 1 teaspoon minced garlic, and ¼ teaspoon of the saffron in a small bowl. Let stand for 5 minutes, then whisk in the mayonnaise and season to taste with salt. Set aside.

2. Heat the remaining 2 tablespoons of olive oil in a deep casserole over medium-high heat. Add the onion and sauté until wilted, then stir in the remaining garlic. Pour in the fish stock and white wine. Stir in the remaining ¼ teaspoon of saffron, the tomato paste, and thyme leaves. Bring the mixture to a boil, then adjust the heat to medium. Add the potato cubes, partially cover, and cook until almost tender, about 12–15 minutes.

3. Stir in the parsley and fish, and cook until the fish is opaque, about 5 minutes. Turn off the heat. Ladle the soup into large, flat bowls. Add 2 slices of toasted baguette to each bowl, if using. Top each with a generous spoonful of aïoli. Serve at once.

*In January it was so nice, While buried under mounds of ice*

*To slurp homemade chicken soup with rice. Slurping once, slurping twice,*

*Three cheers for chicken soup with rice.*

—With apologies to Maurice Sendak, *Chicken Soup with Rice: A Book of Months*

# poultry & meat soups

# Old-Fashioned Chicken Soup with Matzo Balls

*This recipe comes from my dear friend Carole Walter, a world-class baker and, indeed, a Jewish mother par excellence. This is real chicken soup, nectar for the soul, and a magical elixir guaranteed to make you feel better.*

*Using the whole chicken results in a wonderfully rich broth and more than enough cooked chicken for the soup; the leftover chicken can be used in other salads, casseroles, and pot pies, or frozen for future use.*

*It makes sense to make a big batch of soup—enough to serve several ways—including one of three classic chicken soup-carb combinations, with noodles, rice, or, for many, the most comforting of all, matzo balls (recipe follows). The fabled light, fluffy matzo balls are what connoisseurs of this combination crave. What can I say except try it, you'll like it! I can attest to its beneficial attributes (see sidebar).*

*There's one small inconsistency here: the soup recipe makes 3+quarts, whereas the Matzo Ball recipe makes enough for 8 servings. I'm sure you'll figure ways to use the remaining soup, especially since you can freeze it for up to 3 months. It's best to freeze it without the noodles, rice, or matzo balls and add them upon reheating.*

SERVES 12

4–5 pound fowl, capon, or large oven-roaster chicken, quartered

Cold water to cover

4 ribs celery, trimmed and cut in 1- to 2-inch pieces

5–6 carrots, peeled and cut into 2-inch pieces

1 large Spanish onion, studded with 2 cloves

1 large leek, cleaned and sliced

8–10 sprigs fresh dill

8–10 sprigs fresh flat-leaf parsley + 2 tablespoons chopped parsley to garnish

Salt and freshly ground black pepper

Matzo Balls (page 104), cooked noodles, or cooked rice (optional)

1. Put the chicken and giblets in a stockpot. Reserve the liver for another use. Add enough cold water to cover the chicken by 1 inch. Bring to a boil, then reduce the heat to a simmer. Using a skimmer or large spoon, continuously remove the scum as it rises to the surface.

2. Add the celery, carrot, onion, and leek. Simmer for 2 hours or longer, uncovered, until the chicken is tender. Do not allow the broth to boil.

3. Turn off the flame. Tie the dill and parsley together with a string. Add it to the stock and moisten so the flavor is released. Let it stand 20–30 minutes.

4. Have ready a large colander set over a large bowl. Using a slotted spoon, remove the chicken and dill-parsley bouquet to the colander. Pour the stock through a fine strainer into a clean stockpot. Let it stand for ½ hour, then skim off any fat that rises to the surface of the broth.

5. Meanwhile, when the chicken is cool enough to handle, remove the bones and skin, and shred as much of the meat as you want for the soup.

6. Remove the carrots from the cooked vegetables and add them to the strained soup with the shredded chicken meat, as desired. Season to taste with salt and pepper. The soup may be frozen at this point.

7. When ready to serve, add noodles, rice, or matzo balls (see next page) and heat thoroughly. These additions should not stand too long in the soup, as they will absorb too much of the broth. Garnish with chopped parsley.

## NUTRITIONAL INFORMATION

CALORIES 330 | CALORIES FROM FAT 210 | TOTAL FAT 24G | SATURATED FAT 7G

CHOLESTEROL 210MG | TOTAL CARBOHYDRATE 5G | DIETARY FIBER <1G

SUGARS <1G | PROTEIN 23G | VITAMIN A 30% | VITAMIN C 15% | CALCIUM 4% | IRON 10%

* Chicken Matzo Ball Soup to Save My Soul

When I was writing my first article for THE NEW YORK TIMES MAGAZINE, I was also running my cooking school, the Cookingstudio at Kings Super Market, in Short Hills, New Jersey. It was more than a full-time job, plus I had three young kids at home.

One day I called my friend and neighbor Sally Kofke and I told her I felt achy and sick. Within minutes she had her hand on my forehead and, with the aid of a thermometer, told me my fever was above 104°F.

My doctor sent me to bed with a threat that if I didn't stay there, she'd put me in the hospital. While I thought I saw angels dancing on my toes, I kept saying to myself that I needed to stick around to see my article in the TIMES. What hubris!

A few days later, Sally asked if there was something I wanted to eat. I told her that chicken soup with matzo balls was known as "Jewish Penicillin" and surely this golden elixir would help me get better.

No problem, said my good-hearted friend. Now Sally, a good Protestant, had little experience with this particular subject. I think what she brought me was chicken broth with minced chicken breast quenelles.

A day later, when Carole Walter came to visit, I asked if she'd try the soup and—because I knew I was sick—tell me if I just couldn't taste it correctly. Carole said the soup was tasty but it wasn't the magical potion I needed.

Within 24 hours, Carole's penicillin arrived complete with light, fluffy matzo balls, and I got better.

## Matzo Balls

MAKES 18–20 MATZO BALLS

**4 large eggs**

**½ cup club soda**

**3 tablespoons melted chicken fat**

**1 cup matzo meal**

**¾ teaspoon salt**

**2 tablespoons finely chopped flat-leaf parsley**

**Black pepper**

1. Whip the eggs with a handheld mixer until light and foamy. Beat in the club soda and warm chicken fat.

2. Using a whisk, beat in the matzo meal, parsley, and black pepper to taste, stirring continuously until well blended. Cover the bowl with plastic wrap and chill overnight or for at least 6–8 hours.

3. Bring a large pot of salted water to a boil. Have ready a bowl of ice water to moisten your hands. With moistened hands, form the batter into large walnut-sized balls. Drop them into the boiling water and cover the pot. The balls will at least double in size when fully cooked. Boil for 40–45 minutes.

4. When ready to serve, gently reheat the matzo balls in the chicken soup and serve immediately. Do not allow matzo balls to sit too long in the soup, as they will absorb too much of the broth.

**SERVING SIZE: 2 MATZO BALLS**

CALORIES 60 | CALORIES FROM FAT 25 | TOTAL FAT 3G | SATURATED FAT .5G
CHOLESTEROL 40MG | TOTAL CARBOHYDRATE 5G | DIETARY FIBER 0G
SUGARS 0G | PROTEIN 2G | VITAMIN A 0% | VITAMIN C 0% | CALCIUM 0% | IRON 0%

# Chicken Vegetable Alphabet Soup

*When my children were little, I went on a campaign against canned soups filled with lots of salt and chemicals. Try as I might, however, they loved those red-and-white-labeled cans. So, I'd buy them, dump out the contents, and serve my own version, ostensibly from the can. At one point, my daughter Nicole, who has very astute tastebuds, informed me that the soup didn't taste right. In her words, there weren't the "right chemicals." Thank goodness we moved forward.*

SERVES 6–8

2 tablespoons vegetable oil

1 (3-pound) chicken, fat trimmed, cut into pieces, and blotted dry

2 medium carrots, peeled and chopped

2 medium ribs celery, trimmed and chopped

1 large onion, peeled and coarsely chopped

1 large clove garlic, minced

2 cups chicken stock

2 cups water

1 teaspoon dried thyme leaves

1 bay leaf

¼ cup chopped flat-leaf parsley

1 cup frozen peas

1 cup frozen pearl onions

1 cup cooked alphabet pasta

Salt and freshly ground black pepper

1. Heat the oil in a large heavy casserole over medium–high heat until hot. Add only enough chicken as will fit comfortably in the bottom of the pan without crowding, and brown on all sides. Continue until all the pieces are browned. Remove to a plate or bowl and let cool. When cool enough to handle, pull the skin and any excess fat from the chicken.

2. Meanwhile, add the carrots, celery, onion, and garlic to the casserole and cook until lightly browned, 5–6 minutes. Return the chicken to the pan. Add the stock and water, thyme, bay leaf, and parsley. Bring the liquid to a boil, cover the pan, reduce the heat, and let the chicken simmer for 15–20 minutes. Remove the chicken from the soup. Cut the meat from the bones and shred into small pieces.

3. Add the peas, pearl onions, alphabet pasta, chicken, and salt and pepper to taste, and simmer until the vegetables are tender, about 5–6 minutes.

✴ Chicken Options
If you have about 4 cups of leftover diced chicken or a rotisserie chicken, you could use that instead of cooking the bird from scratch.

### NUTRITIONAL INFORMATION

CALORIES 370 | CALORIES FROM FAT 140 | TOTAL FAT 15G | SATURATED FAT 4G

CHOLESTEROL 160MG | TOTAL CARBOHYDRATE 15G | DIETARY FIBER 3G

SUGARS 4G | PROTEIN 42 G | VITAMIN A 50% | VITAMIN C 15% | CALCIUM 8% | IRON 35%

# Greek Chicken & Rice Soup— Avgolemono

*This thick, lemony chicken soup with rice is a classic Greek dish that takes a minimum of effort. It's a perfect rainy-day lunch or even a light supper. My version is slightly more rustic and colorful than some because I leave the minced carrot, onion, and celery in the stock rather than strain them out. Be sure to use fresh lemon juice, as it makes a difference. As with all egg-thickened sauces and soups, it's important not to let the soup boil, or the eggs will curdle.*

SERVES 4–6

1 small onion, peeled

1 small rib celery, trimmed

1 small carrot, scraped

1 tablespoon olive or vegetable oil

2 medium boneless and skinless chicken breast cutlets, cut into ½-inch cubes

4 cups chicken stock

2 tablespoons chopped flat-leaf parsley

⅓ cup raw white rice

2 eggs

4 tablespoon fresh lemon juice

Salt and freshly ground black pepper

1. Mince the onion, celery, and carrots either by hand or in a food processor. If using a processor, pulse the vegetables so you don't over-chop them. Heat the oil in a medium saucepan over medium–high heat. When hot, stir in the onion, celery, and carrot, and sauté until the vegetables are softened, about 5 minutes.

2. Add the chicken, stock, and parsley. Bring the liquid to a boil. Stir in the rice, cover, and reduce the heat so the liquid is barely simmering. Cook until the rice is tender, 20 minutes.

3. Beat the eggs and lemon juice together in a bowl until smooth. Slowly whisk about 1½ cups of the hot broth into the egg-lemon mixture, beating constantly. Stir the warmed egg mixture into the soup. Season to taste with salt and pepper. Heat gently but do not let the liquid boil. Serve at once or keep warm over low heat.

## NUTRITIONAL INFORMATION

CALORIES 220 | CALORIES FROM FAT 70 | TOTAL FAT 8G | SATURATED FAT 1.5G

CHOLESTEROL 130MG | TOTAL CARBOHYDRATE 12G | DIETARY FIBER <1G

SUGARS 1G | PROTEIN 26G | VITAMIN A 40% | VITAMIN C 15% | CALCIUM 4% | IRON 8%

# Curried Turkey & Spinach Soup

*A warming soup, brimming with color and flavor, that takes just minutes to make. It's at its best when eaten right away so the turkey is moist and the spinach is just wilted. As a variation, substitute shrimp or chicken for the turkey; use any other tender green in place of the spinach. This soup is a natural for carbohydrate-restricted diets. However, read the labels on jars of curry paste and mustard to avoid those high in sugar and/or flour.*

1 tablespoon olive oil

1 small onion, peeled and chopped

1 clove garlic, minced

3 tablespoons hot or mild Indian curry paste

6 cups turkey or chicken stock

1½ cups half-and-half

6 tablespoons coarse-grained French mustard

12 ounces uncooked turkey breast, cut into ½-inch cubes

½ pound young spinach leaves

Salt and freshly ground black pepper

SERVES 8

1. Heat the olive oil in a large heavy pot over medium–high heat. Add the onions and garlic and sauté until the onions are wilted and golden in color, 5–6 minutes. Stir in the curry paste, cook for 30 seconds, then whisk in 1 cup of the stock, the half-and-half, and mustard. Transfer to the jar of an electric blender and purée until smooth.

2. Return the mixture to the pot, add the remaining stock, and simmer for 10 minutes, then stir in the turkey and spinach, and cook until the turkey is just cooked through. Season with salt and pepper to taste. Serve at once.

## NUTRITIONAL INFORMATION

CALORIES 190 | CALORIES FROM FAT 90 | TOTAL FAT 10G | SATURATED FAT 3.5G

CHOLESTEROL 50MG | TOTAL CARBOHYDRATE 7G | DIETARY FIBER 4G

SUGARS 0G | PROTEIN 17G | VITAMIN A 40% | VITAMIN C 15% | CALCIUM 15% | IRON 25%

# Penang Curried Rabbit & Spinach in Broth

*This one-dish meal is both visually appealing and exciting (see page 100). It includes pale morsels of juicy rabbit or duck, thin ribbons of spinach, and toothsome, dark japonica rice set against a lushly spicy, pale rose-colored broth. The combination will energize your taste buds.*

*Grains of the California-grown black japonica rice look like polished tiny oval pebbles. They become mahogany colored and densely flavorful when cooked. It is available at many markets and specialty stores.*

SERVES 4

1 tablespoon canola oil

1 young rabbit (2½–3 pounds), or skinless duck or chicken, cut into 8 pieces and blotted dry

Salt and freshly ground black pepper

¾ cup chicken stock

1 (14-ounce) can unsweetened coconut milk

2 tablespoons Penang-style curry paste, available at some supermarkets and Asian markets

2 tablespoons Thai fish sauce (nam pla or nuoc mam)

1 stalk lemongrass, trimmed, center portion finely chopped

2 small hot red chiles, thinly sliced

½ cup black japonica or Thai rice

¾–1 pound spinach, washed, coarse stems removed, and cut crosswise into thin strips

3 tablespoons chopped cilantro

1. Heat the oil in a large, deep skillet over medium–high heat. Add the rabbit, duck, or chicken and brown lightly on both sides, 1–2 minutes. Do not crowd. If necessary, do this in batches. Remove the pieces to a bowl and season generously with salt and pepper.

2. Pour the chicken stock into the skillet and bring to a boil, stirring up all the browned bits. Add the coconut milk, curry paste, fish sauce, lemongrass, and red chiles. Return the rabbit to the pan and simmer gently until tender, about 1 hour. Taste for salt and pepper. If desired, remove the rabbit with a slotted spoon and, when cool enough to handle, cut off the meat from the bones.

3. Meanwhile, bring 1⅛ cups of salted water to a boil. Stir in the rice, cover, and lower the heat so the liquid slowly simmers. Cook until the rice is firm but tender, about 45 minutes.

4. Before serving, stir the spinach into the soup and simmer until just tender. Place a mound of rice in the center of four large flat soup bowls. Divide the rabbit, duck, or chicken among the bowls, ladle on the broth with the spinach, sprinkle on the cilantro, and serve.

# Southwestern Spanish Chorizo & Potato Soup

*A few years ago I traveled to Extremadura, a lovely rustic region in southwestern Spain famous for Iberian ham and hot pimentón de la Vera, finely ground smoked red peppers. The local spicy pork sausage, or chorizo, is also flavored with the peppery powder. Teresa Barrenecha, the Basque-born chef of New York's Marichu Restaurant, was also on the trip and shared this satisfying recipe with me. Chorizo and pimentón are both available on the Internet and at Spanish grocery stores. Pimentón comes in three varieties—sweet, bittersweet, and hot.*

SERVES 4–6

2 tablespoons fragrant olive oil, preferably Spanish + extra to drizzle on

½ cup chopped onion

4 ounces chorizo, casing removed and cut into ¾-inch cubes

1½ pounds baking potatoes, peeled and cut into ¾-inch cubes

2 teaspoons hot pimentón de la Vera or paprika

Salt

4 cups water

1 teaspoon dried oregano

1. Heat the oil in a large casserole over medium heat. Stir in the onion and sauté until just softened, about 5 minutes. Add the sausage and cook until the meat begins to brown, about 2 minutes, stirring often.

2. Add the potatoes, pimentón or paprika, and about a scant teaspoon of salt, and stir well. Pour in the water, raise the heat to high, and bring to a boil. The potatoes should be covered by at least 1 inch of water. Reduce the heat to medium–low, add the oregano, cover, and simmer until the potatoes are tender, about 30 minutes. Taste to adjust the seasonings. Ladle the soup into shallow bowls and serve. If desired, drizzle a little extra olive oil on top of the soup just before serving.

* Chorizo

There are several varieties of chorizo in supermarkets. (The Portuguese version is spelled chourico.) While some are made with chicken, these become dry with cooking. I suggest you use authentic Spanish pork sausages to impart the fullest, most authentic flavor.

## NUTRITIONAL INFORMATION

CALORIES 190 | CALORIES FROM FAT 60 | TOTAL FAT 6G | SATURATED FAT 1G
CHOLESTEROL 10MG | TOTAL CARBOHYDRATE 26G | DIETARY FIBER 2G
SUGARS 2G | PROTEIN 7G | VITAMIN A 6 % | VITAMIN C 25% | CALCIUM 0% | IRON 6%

# Sausage, Kale & Potato Soup

*This stick-to-your-ribs soup is a variation on a classic Portuguese potato-kale soup with linguica. It comes from my dear friend Sally Kofke, an outstanding cook and partner in far too many wonderful meals to recall. It brings back memories of sitting in her kitchen on a bleak winter day and feeling warmed through and through. Following the original recipe is a variation for vegetarians that is also low carb and lactose free.*

SERVES 3–4

¾ pound well-seasoned Italian pork or chicken sausages, casing removed

Olive oil

¼ pounds kale, washed, coarse stems removed, and chopped

1 clove garlic, minced

1½ pounds boiling potatoes, peeled and chopped

½ cup half-and-half

½ cup chicken stock

1 tablespoon balsamic vinegar or 1 tablespoon malt vinegar + 1 teaspoon sugar substitute

Salt and freshly ground black pepper

1. Cook the sausages in a large, deep casserole over medium–high heat until the fat is rendered and the meat is lightly browned, chopping them into pieces with a spatula as they cook. Remove with a slotted spoon, leaving any fat in the pan.

2. Add the kale and garlic to the pan, along with a little olive oil, if needed, and cook over medium heat until the kale is wilted and bright green. Add the half-and-half and stock, cover, and cook until the kale is tender, about 10–15 minutes, stirring occasionally.

3. Meanwhile, put the potatoes in a large pot, cover with cold water, and bring to a boil. Adjust the heat so the water is simmering, cover, and cook until the potatoes are tender, about 20 minutes. Remove from the heat and drain, reserving the cooking water.

4. Return the potatoes to the pot and break them up with a masher. Do not purée, they should still be lumpy. Add about 2 cups of the reserved liquid back to the pot with the potatoes; add the kale and reserved sausage. Bring to a simmer, add the balsamic vinegar, and season to taste with salt and pepper. Ladle into wide bowls and serve.

Vegetarian, low-carb variation without potatoes:

¾ pound well-seasoned Italian-style vegetarian sausages

Olive oil

¼ pounds kale, washed, coarse stems removed, and chopped

1 clove garlic, minced

10 ounces firm tofu, puréed

½ cup soy creamer

½ cup vegetable stock

2 cups soy milk

1 tablespoon balsamic vinegar or
  1 tablespoon malt vinegar +
  1 teaspoon sugar substitute

Salt and freshly ground black pepper

1. Brown the sausages in a little olive oil in a large, deep casserole over medium–high heat, then coarsely chop.

2. Add the kale and garlic, along with a tablespoon of oil, to the pan and cook over medium heat until the kale is wilted and bright green. Pour in the soy creamer and stock, cover, and cook until the kale is tender, about 10–15 minutes, stirring occasionally.

3. Add the puréed tofu and soy milk. Bring to a simmer, add the balsamic vinegar, and season to taste with salt and pepper. Ladle into wide bowls and serve.

### NUTRITIONAL INFORMATION

CALORIES 490 | CALORIES FROM FAT 240 | TOTAL FAT 26G | SATURATED FAT 10G | CHOLESTEROL 75MG | TOTAL CARBOHYDRATE 39G | DIETARY FIBER 5G SUGARS 2G | PROTEIN 25G | VITAMIN A 150% | VITAMIN C 230% | CALCIUM 20% | IRON 25%

### NUTRITIONAL INFORMATION FOR LOW CARB VERSION

CALORIES 240 | CALORIES FROM FAT 50 | TOTAL FAT 6 G | SATURATED FAT 0G | CHOLESTEROL 0MG | TOTAL CARBOHYDRATE 25G | DIETARY FIBER 5G SUGARS 5G | PROTEIN 27G | VITAMIN A 45% | VITAMIN C 45% | CALCIUM 25% | IRON 20%

# Mongolian Hot Pot

*A cross between soup and stew, this satisfying, somewhat piquant one-dish meal takes minutes to finish once the meat is marinated. You can easily change the ingredients and seasonings to your taste. Like other Chinese dishes cooked in a wok, everything should be chopped before you start. Soba (buckwheat) noodles simmered in the broth thicken the soup. If you prefer a thinner soup, add more stock. It's best served shortly after cooking. Otherwise, the noodles absorb a lot of the liquid. If this happens, add more stock or water.*

SERVES 6 AS A MAIN COURSE

¼ cup medium-dry sherry or white grape juice

2½ tablespoons finely grated fresh gingerroot

2 tablespoons soy sauce

2 tablespoons peanut or vegetable oil

1 tablespoon dark brown sugar or sugar substitute

1 tablespoon cornstarch

2 large cloves garlic, crushed

½ teaspoon red pepper flakes

8 ounces flank steak, very thinly sliced across the grain and cut into 1½-inch lengths

1 pound bok choy, thinly sliced crosswise

2 ounces fresh shiitake mushrooms, wiped, stems removed and thinly sliced

4 large scallions, including most of the green parts, thinly sliced

2 medium carrots, peeled and cut into ¼-inch slices

4 cups beef stock

2+ cups water

⅓ cup hoisin sauce

4 ounces soba noodles

Few drops Chinese hot pepper oil (optional)

1. Combine the sherry, ginger, soy sauce, 1 tablespoon of the oil, the brown sugar, garlic, red pepper flakes, and beef in a resealable plastic bag and seal. Turn several times to coat the meat, then marinate 30 minutes at room temperature or refrigerate for up to 24 hours.

2. Heat a large wok over high heat. Add 1 teaspoon of the remaining oil. Lift the beef from marinade with a slotted spoon. Reserve the marinade. Quickly stir-fry the beef until lightly browned on both sides, about 1–2 minutes. Remove from the pan and set aside.

3. Add the remaining oil and stir-fry the bok choy, shiitakes, scallions, and carrots for 1–2 minutes, then add the reserved marinade, stock, water, and hoisin sauce, and bring the mixture to a boil. Stir in the noodles and simmer until tender, about 8–10 minutes. Return the beef to the wok,

cooking long enough to heat through. Finish with a few drops of Chinese hot pepper oil, if desired.

4. Ladle generous portions of the soup into large bowls and serve at once.

### NUTRITIONAL INFORMATION

CALORIES 260 | CALORIES FROM FAT 80 | TOTAL FAT 9G | SATURATED FAT 2G

CHOLESTEROL 15MG | TOTAL CARBOHYDRATE 30G | DIETARY FIBER 3G

SUGARS 3G | PROTEIN 15G | VITAMIN A 120% | VITAMIN C 60% | CALCIUM 10% | IRON 15%

\* Why Use Peanut Oil?
Peanut oil's flame point is higher than almost all other oils, so you can use it to stir-fry foods over very high heat without any problems. However, since it is more fragile than canola or corn oil and becomes rancid rather quickly (not to mention being more expensive), it's best to buy smaller bottles and store them in a cool place.

# Russian Cabbage & Beef Borscht

*Although I first tasted this version of borscht in Paris (see sidebar) the soup originated in Eastern Europe. Typically its base is either beets or meat and cabbage. Beet borscht is generally served cold with generous spoonfuls of sour cream. Cabbage-meat borscht is served hot, sometimes with boiled potatoes added.*

*This classic Old World one-dish meal is incredibly satisfying on a cold winter night. Make it ahead, then share it with family and friends. It gets better as it's reheated. Serve it with thick slices of dark bread.*

SERVES 6–8

2–3 tablespoons vegetable oil

4 pounds meaty beef shin bones, patted dry

Salt and freshly ground pepper

2 large onions, peeled and finely chopped

3 large carrots, peeled and finely chopped

2 large ribs celery, trimmed and finely chopped

2 large cloves garlic, peeled and minced

1 white cabbage (approximately 1½ pounds), cored and shredded

1 (6-ounce) can tomato paste

4 cups warm water

¼ cup chopped flat-leaf parsley

7 cloves

1 large bay leaf

1 teaspoon celery seeds or caraway seeds

2 tablespoons red wine vinegar

2 tablespoons dark brown sugar

½ cup golden raisins (optional)

½ pint sour cream

3 tablespoons freshly chopped dill or 1 tablespoon dried

1. Heat 2 teaspoons of the oil in a very large heavy casserole until very hot. Add only as many pieces of meat as will fit comfortably in the bottom of the pan and cook until richly browned, about 3–4 minutes per side. Remove to a bowl and continue with the remaining meat. Season liberally with salt and pepper and set aside.

2. Add 2 more teaspoons of oil to the pot and, when hot, stir in the onions, carrots, and celery, and sauté over medium–high heat until softened, 4–5 minutes.

3. Add the remaining oil and sauté the garlic and cabbage for 1–2 minutes, stirring frequently. Cover the pot, turn the heat down to medium, and cook the cabbage until wilted, 10 minutes. Uncover the pan, raise the heat to medium–high, and cook for 5–7 minutes longer, turning the vegetables often, until they start to brown.

4. Stir in the tomato paste, water, parsley, cloves, bay leaf, celery seeds, vinegar, brown sugar, raisins, the reserved meat, and a liberal amount of salt and pepper. Bring the liquid to a boil, cover, and adjust the heat down so the liquid is just simmering. Cook gently until the meat is very tender, 2½ –3 hours. Remove the meat from the pan.

5. Skim off any fat on the surface. Cut the meat into chunks, removing the bones, if desired, and return it to the pot. (I usually serve a bone with the marrow to each guest.)

6. Combine the sour cream and dill in a small bowl. Ladle the soup into large bowls, top with a generous dollop of sour cream, and serve. Pass extra sour cream at the table.

**NUTRITIONAL INFORMATION WITH GARNISH**

CALORIES 340 | CALORIES FROM FAT 140 | TOTAL FAT 15G | SATURATED FAT 6G

CHOLESTEROL 90MG | TOTAL CARBOHYDRATE 16G | DIETARY FIBER 4G

SUGARS 9G | PROTEIN 36G | VITAMIN A 100% | VITAMIN C 60% | CALCIUM 10% | IRON 20%

* A Parisian Discovery

Having moved to Paris shortly after graduating from college, I soon found myself in need of work and money. It was March, and the City of Light was cold and damp. A kindly photographer I'd met through friends suggested I come to his studio to have some pictures taken, with the thought that I might find some luck with modeling. (I had no such illusions, however, but went anyway.)

As we were shooting the photos, I smelled the most intoxicating aroma coming from his kitchen. When he invited me to join him and his wife for lunch, I jumped at the opportunity. We sat down to hearty bowls of sweet-and-sour cabbage soup, rich with tender chunks of meat and topped with generous spoonfuls of dill-flecked sour cream. It was incredibly satisfying.

Some years later, while visiting my father in California, I prepared my version of the soup as I remembered it. He burst out laughing and said, "So you had to go to Paris to discover a Russian peasant dish!"

# Earthy Lamb & Lentil Soup

*This robust soup is an ideal antidote to any cold, blustery day. It keeps well for at least a week in the refrigerator and gets even better with reheating. Although there is a minimum of meat, the lamb imparts plenty of flavor.*

SERVES 4–6

1 large onion, peeled

1 large carrot, peeled

1 medium rib celery, trimmed

1 large clove garlic, split

2 teaspoons vegetable oil

1 lamb shank, patted dry

2 cups chicken stock

2 tablespoons chopped flat-leaf parsley

1 teaspoon fresh thyme leaves or
½ teaspoon dried thyme leaves

1 bay leaf

1 cup dried lentils, rinsed and picked
over for foreign particles

4 cups water

Salt and freshly ground black pepper

1–2 tablespoons sherry vinegar or apple
cider vinegar

1. Finely chop the onions, carrots, celery, and garlic. If using a processor, pulse the vegetables so you don't over-chop them.

2. Heat 3 teaspoons of the oil in a very large heavy pot over medium–high heat. Stir in the vegetables and sauté until almost wilted, about 4 minutes, stirring occasionally. Move the vegetables aside and add the remaining teaspoon of oil to the pot. Add the lamb shank and lightly brown on all sides. Stir the vegetables often to prevent burning.

3. Pour in the stock and stir up any browned cooking bits. Add the parsley, thyme, bay leaf, and lentils. Add about 1 cup of the water. Cover the pot, bring the liquid to a boil, then reduce the heat so the liquid simmers. Cook until the lentils and lamb are very tender, about 45–50 minutes. Discard the bay leaf. Remove the lamb shank and, when cool enough to handle, cut the meat from bone and chop into small pieces. Set aside

4. Transfer the lentil mixture in batches to a food processor and pulse until it is chunky–smooth. Return the soup and lamb to the pot. Stir in the remaining water. Season to taste with salt and pepper and heat until very hot. Just before serving, stir in the vinegar.

### NUTRITIONAL INFORMATION

CALORIES 280 | CALORIES FROM FAT 80 | TOTAL FAT 8G | SATURATED FAT 2.5G

CHOLESTEROL 30MG | TOTAL CARBOHYDRATE 34G | DIETARY FIBER 6G

SUGARS 4G | PROTEIN 18G | VITAMIN A 90% | VITAMIN C 15% | CALCIUM 4% | IRON 15%

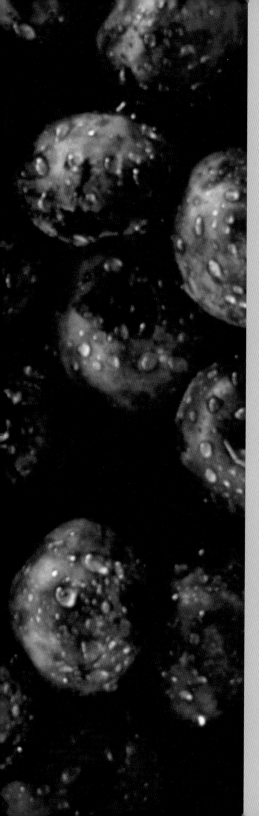

At Villa Vespa, in Lake Placid, New York,

*Waitresses offered melon or soup as a starter.*

*Guests continuously combined the two, ordering "melon soup."*

*So chef Kimberly Vespa added chilled cantaloupe soup to the menu.*

# fruit soups

# Curried Mango Soup with Lobster

*Purée mangoes with coconut milk, Penang red curry paste, ginger, and lemongrass. Add lobster and fresh mango/red pepper/basil salsa and both your eyes and tastebuds will be seduced. If you like spicy foods, add finely diced hot red chilies to the salsa. The soup itself has a nice hot-sweet taste.*

SERVES 4

1 cup puréed ripe mango (see sidebar)

1 cup aseptically packaged mango nectar (not canned mango pulp)

1 cup canned unsweetened coconut milk

2 tablespoons Penang-style red curry paste, available at some supermarkets and Asian groceries

1 tablespoon finely chopped fresh lemongrass

1-inch piece of fresh gingerroot, peeled

1 tablespoon light brown sugar

1 tablespoon unsalted butter

8 ounces lobster meat, cut into ½-inch cubes, or 12 ounces diced firm tofu

2 tablespoons dark rum (optional)

Salt and freshly ground black pepper

Mango Salsa (recipe follows)

1. Combine the puréed mango, mango nectar, coconut milk, curry paste, lemongrass, gingerroot, and brown sugar in the jar of an electric blender and blend until completely smooth. Pour the soup through a fine strainer, pressing to extract as much liquid as possible, into a bowl.

2. Heat the butter in a large skillet over medium–high heat. Add the lobster and sauté until just cooked through, 1–2 minutes, turning frequently. Season to taste with salt and pepper. Pour on the rum, if using, and cook over high heat for 30 seconds. Scrape into the soup.

3. Divide the soup among four large, flat soup bowls. Top each with a generous spoonful of Mango Salsa and serve.

## Mango Salsa

½ cup finely diced ripe mango

½ cup finely diced red bell pepper or a combination of bell pepper and hot red chile peppers

2 tablespoons finely chopped basil

1 tablespoon fresh lime juice

1. Combine the mango, red pepper, basil, and lime juice in a bowl.

* Sweet Dreams Of Mango Soup
Inspired by a "foodie movie," I dreamed up this curried mango soup with coconut milk. I wanted to capture the exquisite perfume the fruit has when grown in tropical climates and play it against red Thai curry and sweet lobster meat.

Unfortunately, while most of what we find in our markets may get soft, it never develops that lush floral taste. To compensate, I combine the ripest mangoes I can find (usually not the prettiest ones) with some aseptically packaged mango nectar. If you are lucky enough to have tree-ripe mangoes, I'm jealous.

**NUTRITIONAL INFORMATION**

CALORIES 320 | CALORIES FROM FAT 150 | TOTAL FAT 16G | SATURATED FAT 13G

CHOLESTEROL 60MG | TOTAL CARBOHYDRATE 29G | DIETARY FIBER 2G

SUGARS 21G | PROTEIN 12G | VITAMIN A 60% | VITAMIN C 80% | CALCIUM 6% | IRON 6%

# Peach Soup with Blueberries

*For anyone who doesn't want to cook on a sultry summer day, here's a refreshing dessert that will tease and please you and your guests. It takes a minimum of work on your part. Fresh blueberries set off the smooth peach soup. To dress it up, serve a tiny scoop of peach sorbet on top and garnish with small mint leaves. Be sure to use low- or full-fat yogurt rather than the nonfat variety; otherwise, this soup will taste too thin.*

SERVES 4

2–3 large ripe peaches, peel and stone removed, puréed (about 1 cup) and refrigerated until very cold

1 cup apple cider

2 tablespoons honey

1 tablespoon fresh lemon juice

½ teaspoon ground nutmeg

6 ounces vanilla yogurt

½ pint fresh blueberries

Peach sorbet (optional)

Mint leaves, to garnish

1. Combine the peaches, cider, honey, lemon juice, and nutmeg in the bowl of an electric blender and purée until smooth. Pour into a bowl, fold in the yogurt, then cover, and chill for at least 2 hours.

2. Before serving, stir in the blueberries, ladle the soup into bowls, add a small scoop of sorbet, and garnish with a mint leaf.

**NUTRITIONAL INFORMATION**

CALORIES 150 | CALORIES FROM FAT 10 | TOTAL FAT 1G | SATURATED FAT 0.5G

CHOLESTEROL <5MG | TOTAL CARBOHYDRATE 29G | DIETARY FIBER 3G

SUGARS 24G | PROTEIN 3G | VITAMIN A 10% | VITAMIN C 20% | CALCIUM 6% | IRON 2%

# Cantaloupe Soup

*Purée ripe melons with small amounts of sour cream, Cassis, and chopped mint leaves for this soup. Each bowl is served with a dab of sour cream and a fresh mint leaf for a delightful hot-weather soup. For a more complex taste, I sometimes add a couple of tablespoons of minced prosciutto. That little hint of salt makes the other tastes sparkle.*

SERVES 6

2 large ripe cantaloupes, peeled and
  puréed until smooth (about 5 cups pulp)

1 cup low-fat sour cream +
  2 tablespoons for garnish

½ cup Cassis

¼ cup chopped mint leaves + fresh mint
  leaves for garnish

1. Blend the cantaloupe, sour cream, and Cassis together in the bowl until smooth. Stir in the chopped mint leaves, cover, and chill until very cold. Chill the bowls, as well.

2. Ladle the soup into the bowls, add a teaspoon of sour cream, a mint leaf, and serve.

**NUTRITIONAL INFORMATION**

CALORIES 150 | CALORIES FROM FAT 50 | TOTAL FAT 5G | SATURATED FAT 3G

CHOLESTEROL 15MG | TOTAL CARBOHYDRATE 18G | DIETARY FIBER 2G

SUGARS 12G | PROTEIN 3G | VITAMIN A 15% | VITAMIN C 45% | CALCIUM 8% | IRON 6%

# Spiced Plum-Cherry Soup

SMART FAT
LOW CALORIE
VEGETARIAN OR VEGAN

*Hidden within this dark plummy-colored soup is a lush blend of exotic spices that make this a seductive finale for any meal. I serve it with cookies or even chocolate brownies. Since the softened plums are strained, you do not need to peel or pit them before cooking.*

SERVES 4–5

¾ cup ripe red plums, split

¾ cup unsweetened pomegranate juice

10 black peppercorns

6 whole cloves

1 star anise

1 cinnamon stick

¼ teaspoon whole fennel seeds

2 tablespoons honey

1 (12-ounce) package frozen dark sweet pitted cherries, defrosted or ¾ pound fresh

2–4 ounces sour cream or soy yogurt, to garnish

1 tablespoon finely julienned orange zest

1. Combine the plums, pomegranate juice, peppercorns, cloves, anise, cinnamon, and fennel seeds in a small heavy saucepan and bring the liquid to a boil. Cover, turn the heat down so the liquid gently boils, and cook until the plums are very soft, 40 minutes. Turn off the heat and let the mixture cool with the spices.

2. Discard the cinnamon. Pour the soup through a fine strainer, pressing to extract as much liquid as possible. You should have about 2½ cups.

3. Stir in the honey and the cherries.

4. To serve, ladle about ½ cup of soup into four small bowls. Fill a plastic squeeze-bottle with sour cream and make decorative dots, squiggles, or a crosshatch pattern on the top. Sprinkle a pinch of orange zest in the center and serve.

## NUTRITIONAL INFORMATION

CALORIES 180 | CALORIES FROM FAT 35 | TOTAL FAT 4G | SATURATED FAT 2G

CHOLESTEROL 5MG | TOTAL CARBOHYDRATE 35G | DIETARY FIBER 4G

SUGARS 31G | PROTEIN 2G | VITAMIN A 6% | VITAMIN C 35% | CALCIUM 6% | IRON 6%

# Minted Watermelon Soup

SMART FAT

LOW CALORIE

VEGETARIAN OR VEGAN

*A refreshingly cool summer soup with a pleasant tang. It's the epitome of simplicity: ripe, luscious watermelon, tangy buttermilk, and mint. To make a decorative tureen, hollow out the rounded end of the melon—about 8 inches in length—and fill it with the delicate pink liquid flecked with green.*

*Although you can find buttermilk that is only ½ percent butterfat, look for one with at least 1 ½ percent.*

SERVES 6

5 ½–6 pounds watermelon, peeled and seeded

1 ½ cups buttermilk (see above), plain yogurt, or soy yogurt

3 tablespoons chopped fresh mint leaves + small leaves to garnish

1 cup tiny watermelon balls or mixed melon balls

1. Purée enough melon in a food processor until you have about 5 cups. This should be done in batches. Transfer it to a large bowl, stir in the buttermilk and mint, cover, and chill for at least 2 hours.

2. Make the melon tureen, if desired, and add the soup and melon balls. Ladle the soup into bowls, garnish with mint leaves, and serve.

## NUTRITIONAL INFORMATION

CALORIES 180 | CALORIES FROM FAT 25 | TOTAL FAT 2.5G | SATURATED FAT 0.5G

CHOLESTEROL <5MG | TOTAL CARBOHYDRATE 37G | DIETARY FIBER 2G

SUGARS 46G | PROTEIN 5G | VITAMIN A 35% | VITAMIN C % | CALCIUM 10% | IRON 4%

*Garnishes must be matched like a tie to a suit.*

—Fernand Point, *Ma gastronomie*

*Condiments are like old friends—highly thought of, but often taken for granted.*

—Marilyn Kaytor, *Look* magazine, 1963

# garnishes, condiments & other tasty additions

# Individual Bread Soup Bowls

*A fun way to serve soup is in individual edible bowls. Save the bread you pull out and use it for croutons.*

SERVES 4

**4 (8-ounce) round, firm-textured rolls,**
  **such as whole-grain or sourdough**

**4 tablespoons unsalted butter, melted**

1. Preheat your oven to 350°F. Slice about ¾ inch off the top of each roll. Scoop out the inside bread, leaving about a ½-inch-thick shell.

2. Liberally brush the insides of the rolls and lids with melted butter or a mixture of melted butter and olive oil. Put the bowls and lids, buttered-side up, directly on the oven rack, and bake until crisp, about 20 minutes. Remove and set aside to cool. Fill the soup bowls just before serving so they don't become soggy.

\* Everybody Loves Croutons

Almost everyone loves croutons in soups. The word "crouton" comes from the French word croûte, which means crust. And like a good crust, crispy croutons—as opposed to soggy ones—are preferable for textural interest.

I like to use small cubes or slightly larger, irregular pieces of firm-textured bread. French bread, sourdough, multi-grain, and even pumpernickel croutons are great complements to hearty soups. Day-old loaves or slices are great because they aren't very porous.

Toss the cut-up bread with a little oil or melted butter, or a combination of both. You can also infuse the oil with garlic and herbs. Bake croutons on a cookie sheet in a 375°F oven or sauté them in a large skillet until crisp, turning to brown on all sides. Sometimes I sprinkle a little finely grated cheese over them when they are almost cooked and let it melt.

**NUTRITIONAL INFORMATION**

CALORIES 570 | CALORIES FROM FAT 120 | TOTAL FAT 13G | SATURATED FAT 8G
CHOLESTEROL 35MG | CARBOHYDRATES 95G | DIETARY FIBER 5G | PROTEIN 16G

# Parmesan-Black Pepper Crisps

6 tablespoons freshly shredded
  Parmigiano-Reggiano cheese

¼ teaspoon coarsely ground black pepper

1. Combine the cheese and black pepper in a bowl. Heat a large nonstick skillet over medium–high heat.

2. For each crisp, sprinkle 1 tablespoon of cheese in a 3-inch circle. It should be thin. Leave about 2 inches between the circles. Cook until the cheese melts and the edges begin to brown. Remove with a spatula and cool on a cake rack.

## NUTRITIONAL INFORMATION FOR 1 CRISP

CALORIES 50 | CALORIES FROM FAT 30 | TOTAL FAT 3G | SATURATED FAT 2G

CHOLESTEROL 5MG | CARBOHYDRATES 0G | DIETARY FIBER 0G | SUGAR 0G | PROTEIN 2G

# Rosemary-Parmesan Crostini with Variations

*In Tuscany, crostini are little slices of Tuscan bread spread with a topping and often served as an hors d'oeuvre. The combination of rosemary bread—a traditional rustic bread most likely found at Italian or other artisanal bakeries—and Parmesan cheese is one of my favorite partners for soups. If you can't find rosemary bread, use a firm baguette or dense Tuscan-style bread. Thin strands of freshly shredded Parmigiano-Reggiano add the best flavor, but other hard grating cheeses will also work.*

7 (¼ -inch) slices stale rosemary or other firm-textured bread, cut in half

1–2 teaspoons extra-virgin olive oil

1 clove garlic, split

3 tablespoons freshly shredded Parmigiano-Reggiano

MAKES 14 SLICES

1. Turn on the broiler, positioning the rack about 5 inches from the heat. Lightly brush one side of each slice with olive oil and rub with garlic. Place the slices oiled-side up on a baking sheet and broil just until lightly browned, 2 minutes.

2. Remove the pan from the oven, turn, brush the second side with oil, rub again with garlic, and then sprinkle cheese over the slices. Broil until the cheese is bubbling and golden brown, about 2½ minutes more, checking often so they don't burn.

**NUTRITIONAL INFORMATION FOR 1 SLICE**

CALORIES 50 | CALORIES FROM FAT 20 | TOTAL FAT 2.5G | SATURATED FAT .5G
CHOLESTEROL 0G | DIETARY FIBER 0G | SUGAR 0G | PROTEIN 2G

**✳ Favorite Combinations**
Another great crostini combination is shredded Asiago cheese and minced fresh sage leaves melted on multi-grain bread slices. Of course, Gruyère or Parmesan on sourdough baguettes is also pretty terrific—you can replace the oil with butter and leave out the garlic if you wish.

# Chili-Crusted Pumpkin Seeds

*If you're like me, you'll probably nibble these tasty seeds even when you're not serving soup. They're great for cocktail parties, but they really shine when sprinkled on hot soups. The crunchy morsels are a good source of iron and zinc.*

1 cup raw hulled pumpkin seeds

1 teaspoon vegetable oil

2 teaspoons hot or mild chili powder

½ teaspoon ground cumin

½ teaspoon salt

Pinch cayenne pepper

1. Preheat your oven to 350°F. Toss the seeds with the oil, chili powder, cumin, salt, and cayenne. Spread them on a lightly oiled baking sheet and cook for 25–30 minutes, turning occasionally. Remove and let cool. Store in an airtight container. They will keep for at least a month.

**NUTRITIONAL INFORMATION FOR 1 TABLESPOON**

CALORIES 80 | CALORIES FROM FAT 70 | TOTAL FAT 8G | SATURATED FAT 1.5G
CHOLESTEROL 0G | CARBOHYDRATES 2G | DIETARY FIBER 0 | SUGAR 0 | PROTEIN 4G

# Marinated Tofu

*A tasty addition and visual complement to any puréed soup, tofu is an excellent source of low-fat protein. Change the herb to flatter the soup's flavors.*

¼ pound firm tofu, cut into tiny cubes

3 tablespoons fruity extra-virgin olive oil

1 teaspoon fresh thyme leaves

Pinch salt

1. Blend the tofu, olive oil, thyme and salt in a bowl and let marinate for at least 10 minutes. Spoon 1-2 tablespoons of tofu on the surface of each bowl of soup.

**NUTRITIONAL INFORMATION FOR 1 TABLESPOON**

CALORIES 40 | CALORIES FROM FAT 40 | TOTAL FAT 4G | SATURATED FAT .5G
CHOLESTEROL 0G | CARBOHYDRATES 0 | DIETARY FIBER 0 | SUGAR 0 | PROTEIN <1G

# Basil Pesto

*Pesto can impart a big boost of flavor to simple soups. While basil pesto is easy to make, it's also readily available in supermarkets and specialty food stores. Sadly, many commercial pestos aren't very good; taste first before adding them to anything. The best ones are sold refrigerated. Try the Lemon-Parsley Pesto on page 92 or create your own blend of herbs, sun-dried tomatoes, and even artichoke hearts using this basic model.*

2 cups loosely packed basil leaves

1-2 large cloves garlic

4 tablespoons pine nuts, lightly toasted

3 tablespoons extra-virgin olive oil

2 tablespoons unsalted butter, at room temperature, or use all olive oil

½ teaspoon salt

½ cup freshly grated Parmigiano-Reggiano cheese

1. Combine the basil, garlic, pine nuts, olive oil, butter, and salt in the jar of a blender or food processor, and purée until almost smooth. Scrape into a bowl, stir in the cheese, and set aside. Spoon dollops in the center of a bowl of soup.

## NUTRITIONAL INFORMATION FOR 1 TABLESPOON

CALORIES 60 | CALORIES FROM FAT 50 | TOTAL FAT 6G | SATURATED FAT 2G
CHOLESTEROL 5MG | CARBOHYDRATES 0 | DIETARY FIBER 0 | SUGAR 0 | PROTEIN 1G

# Herbed Tortilla Crisps

*Vary the flavor of the tortilla, the herb, and even the cheese to complement your soup.*

2 (12-inch) flour tortillas

1 tablespoon vegetable oil

¼ teaspoon dried oregano

1 tablespoon grated Parmesan cheese,
  optional

YIELDS 4–6 SERVINGS

1. Preheat the broiler with rack positioned about 5 inches from the heat.

2. Lightly brush the tortillas with oil, sprinkle on the oregano and Parmesan cheese, if using, then cut the tortillas into ¾- x 2-inch wide strips. Bake on a baking sheet until crisp and lightly browned, 3–4 minutes. These may be done ahead of time and stored in a loosely covered container.

**NUTRITIONAL INFORMATION FOR ½ OUNCE**

CALORIES 60 | CALORIES FROM FAT 30 | TOTAL FAT 3.5G | SATURATED FAT .5G

CHOLESTEROL 0 | CARBOHYDRATES 7G | DIETARY FIBER 0G | SUGAR 0G | PROTEIN 1G

*Stock is everything in cooking.... If one's stock is good, what remains of the work is easy.*

—George Auguste Escoffier, "Guide Culinaire"

# basic stock recipes

# Chicken Stock

*This makes a lot of chicken stock. You can cut the recipe in half, if you like. But if you use chicken stock as often as I do, it's just as easy to make a large quantity as a small amount. I then freeze it for future use. To make turkey stock, use the cooked turkey carcass, broken into pieces, and add the uncooked wingtips and neck, if you have them, to the stockpot.*

MAKES ABOUT 4 QUARTS

10 pounds uncooked chicken carcasses, wings, backs, and ribs, chopped into 1½-inch pieces (see note)

3 large carrots, coarsely chopped

3 large unpeeled onions, quartered

2 large ribs celery including leaves, coarsely chopped

6 large sprigs flat-leaf parsley

10 black peppercorns

3 bay leaves

1 tablespoon salt

1½ gallons water

1. Combine the chicken, carrots, onions, celery, parsley, peppercorns, bay leaves, and salt in a large, deep stockpot. Add enough water to cover the chicken, about 1½ gallons. Bring the water to just below the boiling point over high heat, then reduce the heat so the liquid is gently simmering. Partially cover and cook for 2–2½ hours, skimming off any scum that rises to the surface, then let cool.

2. When cool, strain the stock through cheesecloth. Do not press on the solids, or the stock will become cloudy. Discard the bones, herbs, and vegetables. Cover and refrigerate for up to 3 days, or freeze for 5–6 months. Skim off the congealed surface fat before using.

NOTE: Get in the habit of saving raw chicken parts, like wings, backs, and ribs, each time you cut up a chicken. Some markets sell these for a nominal amount of money. Put them into a resealable plastic bag or container and store in the freezer until you have a sufficient amount to make stock. Even cooked carcasses add flavor to stock. Break them into pieces and add them to the pot.

* Broth versus Stock

Many soup recipes call for adding "broth." Others say "stock" is the liquid to use. There seems to be a general confusion between the terms, and often they are used interchangeably.

For the purposes of this book, I have used the word stock throughout the ingredient lists with the notion that it is a liquid derived from simmering meaty bones of animals, poultry, or fish trimmings along with aromatic vegetables and seasonings (or simply vegetables and their trimmings for a vegetable stock). It is then used as the foundation for other soups.

The difference between brown and light stocks is that for the former, usually the bones are browned in a hot oven or over a flame, combined with aromatic vegetables, and water and sometimes wine. For a light-colored stock, the bones are boiled in water, skimmed, and not browned.

The term "bouillon" is also used to describe clear liquids made by boiling meats or poultry and seasonings in water. However, if you are serious about soup making, don't think about using bouillon cubes. These evaporated squares are rich in salt and chemical tastes and won't enhance your soups.

145

# Rich Brown Chicken Stock

*For a robust-tasting chicken stock, use this version. As with meat stock, you can similarly reduce it down to a demi-glace by boiling it until you have about 2 cups of liquid. It will last for 3–4 days in the refrigerator or for six months in the freezer.*

MAKES 2 QUARTS

3 pounds chicken carcasses or wings, backs, and ribs, chopped into 1½-inch pieces (see note on page 144)

2 medium ribs celery including leaves, chopped

1 medium carrot, peeled and chopped

1 onion, peeled and chopped

5 garlic cloves, split in half

1 tomato, chopped

1 tablespoon tomato paste

½ cup white wine

2 quarts water

2 bay leaves

5 sprigs flat-leaf parsley

4 sprigs thyme

Salt and pepper

1. Put the bones in a large deep skillet and cook over medium–high heat until golden brown, turning occasionally. Add the celery, carrot, onion, and garlic, and cook until the vegetables are golden brown, 7–8 minutes.

2. Stir in the tomato and tomato paste, cook for 5 minutes, then pour in the white wine and cook for 2 minutes more. Add the water, bay leaves, parsley, and thyme. Simmer for 1 hour, skimming the surface from time to time. Pour the liquid through a fine strainer into a clean pot. Season to taste with salt and pepper to taste. If needed, reduce over high heat to the desired taste and consistency.

\* Making the Mundane Better

To enrich a weak or canned stock, add 1 medium rib of celery, chopped; ½ small onion, chopped; 1 small carrot, chopped; a couple sprigs of parsley; and a couple of black pepper-corns to 3½ cups (2 cans) of stock. Bring the liquid to a boil, then lower the heat and boil gently until the liquid has reduced to 2 cups, about 15–20 minutes, then strain.

# Rich Duck Stock

3 pounds duck bones, chopped into
  pieces (see note)

2 tablespoons vegetable oil

1 cup each thinly sliced onion, carrot,
  and celery

2 teaspoons salt

2 quarts water

4 sprigs flat-leaf parsley

2 sprigs fresh thyme

2 bay leaves

1 large clove garlic, unpeeled

10 black peppercorns

MAKES ABOUT 2 QUARTS

1. Preheat the oven to 375°F.

2. Spread the bones on a heavy baking sheet. Drizzle on the oil, tossing to
coat. Roast for 30 minutes, turning occasionally. Add the onion, carrots,
and celery, turn to coat with oil, and roast until the vegetables are richly
browned but not scorched, about 25 minutes.

3. Transfer the bones and vegetables into a large saucepan, deglazing the
pan with enough hot water to dissolve all the browned spots. Add to the
stock. Add salt and 8 cups of water, or more if needed to cover bones. Bring
the liquid to a boil, then adjust heat down so the liquid is simmering fairly
quickly. Simmer for 45 minutes, skimming any fat and impurities that rise
to the surface.

4. Add the parsley, thyme, bay leaves, garlic, and peppercorns. Simmer for 3
hours, adding hot water as necessary to keep the bones and vegetables covered. Pour through a fine sieve, pressing with a wooden spoon to extract as
much liquid as possible. Pour through a strainer lined with several layers of
dampened cheesecloth. If there are more than 8 cups, boil to reduce the stock.

NOTE: Making duck stock is simple only if you have access to a butcher who cuts up whole
ducks or you buy whole birds and use only the breasts. Otherwise, substitute chicken stock.
Or, for a light Duck Stock, you could forgo roasting the bones and make a simple duck stock
the same way as with a chicken carcass, by putting the remains of the carved roast bird into
a pot with water.

# Meat Stock

*This flavorful beef stock is the basis for wonderful soups, stews, and sauces. If reduced by half, it becomes demi-glace. Reduced to a thick, gelatinous consistency—about a quarter of its original volume—it's known as glace de viande or meat glaze. At that point, the flavor is very intense. A little of this "amber gold" added to any dish would dramatically enrich the flavor. Stock keeps for 3 days in the refrigerator or for 5–6 months frozen.*

MAKES ABOUT 3 QUARTS

2½ pounds raw beef bones with some meat (shin, marrow, ribs), cracked if large

1½ pounds meaty raw veal shanks or knuckles, cracked if large

3 medium carrots, cut in 2-inch lengths

2 large unpeeled onions, split with 1 clove stuck in each half

1 leek or the green tops of 2 leeks, trimmed, rinsed, and split in half lengthwise

1 large rib celery including leaves, cut in 2-inch lengths

4+ quarts cold water

½ cup warm water

3 sprigs flat-leaf parsley

2 sprigs fresh thyme or 1 teaspoon dried

1 large unpeeled clove garlic, split

5 black peppercorns

½ teaspoon salt, optional (see note)

1. Preheat the oven to 400°F.

2. Put the beef and veal bones in a large, shallow roasting pan and roast until browned on all sides, turning occasionally, 45 minutes to 1 hour. Pour off almost all the fat.

3. Add the carrots, onions, cut-side down, leek, and celery to the pan and roast until the vegetables have started to brown and caramelize, about 15 minutes longer.

4. Transfer the bones and vegetables to a large stockpot, add the cold water, and bring just to a boil. Adjust the heat down so the liquid is simmering. Skim off any scum that rises to the surface during the first hour.

5. Meanwhile, deglaze the roasting pan with the warm water, scraping up all the browned cooking bits with a wooden spoon, and add this liquid to the stockpot.

6. Stir in the parsley, thyme, garlic, peppercorns, and salt, if using. Partially cover and simmer for at least 8 hours, adding water if needed to cover the ingredients.

7. Strain the stock into a large bowl or bowls, cover, and refrigerate overnight. Skim off the layer of fat on the surface and discard.

8. Refrigerate or freeze the stock until needed. Or, return it to the pot, bring it to a boil, and boil rapidly to reduce it to a demi-glace or *glace de viande*. As the stock thickens, adjust the heat to low and watch to make sure it doesn't burn. Refrigerated glace de viande lasts for several days. Cut into cubes and frozen in small resealable plastic bags, it keeps for about 5–6 months. You may also pour it into ice cube trays, cover it tightly, and use cubes as you need them.

NOTE: Vegetables and meat have a certain amount of natural salt. If you plan on making glace de viande, no additional salt is needed.

# Fish Stock

*Fish stock is like court bouillon that is used to poach fish, except rather than cooking a whole fish in the liquid, you use the trimmings and bones from two to three lean white, non-oily fish. Store in the refrigerator for 3–4 days or freeze for 3 months.*

MAKES ABOUT 2 QUARTS

1½ quarts water

2 cups dry white wine

⅓ cup white wine vinegar

2 medium onions, each stuck with 3 whole cloves

2 medium carrots, coarsely chopped

1 large rib celery with leaves, coarsely chopped

3 sprigs flat-leaf parsley

1 sprig thyme

1 bay leaf

½ tablespoon salt

Trimmings and uncooked bones from 2–3 lean white, non-oily fish

1. Combine the water, wine, vinegar, onions, carrots, celery, parsley, thyme, bay leaf, and salt in a large pot and bring to a boil. Add the fish, turn the heat down so the liquid is simmering, cover, and cook for 1–1½ hours.

2. Strain the stock through several layers of cheesecloth. Taste to adjust the seasonings and reduce the stock over high heat if needed.

# Vegetable Stock

*One of the easiest ways to collect fixings for vegetable stock is to get in the habit of keeping vegetable trimmings including onion skins; carrot, turnip, and potato peelings; and those wonderful dark green tops of leeks and celery hearts. Lots of chefs use papery onion skins in their stocks since these add color. The trick is to keep all the fixings in good condition. Unless you gather them within a day or two, it's best to freeze them in a resealable plastic bag, with all the air squeezed out, until you have a sizable quantity. Then, defrost them and add them to the recipe below. My vegetable stock differs each time I make it. What follows is a general plan. Don't forget lots of onions and garlic.*

1 tablespoon vegetable oil

5 large carrots, coarsely chopped

3 large onions, coarsely chopped

3 large ribs celery including leaves, coarsely chopped

2 large leeks, trimmed, rinsed, and split in half lengthwise

2 large cloves garlic, split

Leftover vegetable trimmings, including bell peppers, turnips, onion skins, tomatoes, etc., defrosted if frozen

2 quarts water

½ cup warm water

4 large sprigs flat-leaf parsley

3 sprigs thyme leaves

1 bay leaf

Salt and black pepper

MAKES ABOUT 2 QUARTS

1. Preheat your oven to 375°F. Brush a large, flat roasting pan with oil.

2. Scatter the chopped vegetables and garlic in the pan, turning to coat them with the oil, and roast until they begin to brown. Add the defrosted trimmings and continue cooking until the vegetables are a rich, dark golden brown, turning often, about 40–55 minutes depending on the size. Be sure they don't burn.

3. Remove the pan from the oven and transfer the vegetables to a deep pot. Add the 2 quarts of water, parsley, thyme, and bay leaf, and bring to a boil.

4. Meanwhile, stir the warm water into the roasting pan, scraping up the browned cooking bits with a wooden spoon, and add it to the pot. Cover and simmer until the vegetables are very soft, 1–1½ hours.

5. Strain the stock through cheesecloth into a clean pot. Season to taste with salt and pepper and, if desired, reduce further. Cool and refrigerate until needed. It will keep for 3–4 days in the refrigerator, or up to 3 months frozen in airtight containers.

\* Mushroom Stock
Each time you reconstitute dried wild mushrooms, strain the liquid through paper towels or a fine sieve, reduce it in a small saucepan or in the microwave down to a syrupy liquor, and freeze it. You can add layer upon layer to the jar; just boil it before reusing it. You'll be amazed how the smallest amount can lushly perfume a sauce, soup, or stew.

# Wine and Other Drinks to Accompany Soups

People often say they are confused about the appropriate drink to serve with soups. Like most food-wine pairings, I think personal preference should play a large part in the choice. In reality, a broad variety of drinks partner well with soups—including wine, sherry and other fortified wines, cider, beer, some teas and, of course, water. If you are willing to experiment, you may be pleasantly surprised at how exciting these pairings can be.

That being said, what follows are some personal guidelines that I hope you'll find helpful.

For starters, I think about the flavor and texture of a soup and generally hold with a "like takes to like" approach. For example, if a soup is prepared with red wine or is meaty, such as Russian Cabbage & Beef Borscht, it seems natural to serve a robust red wine. While the choices are vast, including reasonably priced bottles of Cabernet Sauvignon, Chianti, and Merlot from many countries, remember that inferior-tasting wines used in cooking *never* improve in taste nor flatter the other ingredients.

Spicy soups made with ingredients like chorizo or kielbasa also need a sturdy, spicy complement, such as a good Rhône or Shiraz. Many of the South African reds that recently have become available here really flatter the smoky flavors of ham, sausage, and bacon.

For soups with cheese, such as those made with Gruyère or Emmenthaler, a lighter red, like Beaujolais, is appealing. Or try an Alsatian Pinot Blanc with earthy, complex flavors and lighter body.

When a recipe calls for dry white wine, such as Jerusalem Artichoke Soup with Marinated Tofu, again it's logical to serve the same wine. I often pair California Sauvignon Blanc or French Entre-deux-Mers with light vegetable-based soups. Fresh, slightly tingly but complex-tasting Spanish Albariños are a wonderful complement to light fish soups, especially those with grilled shellfish.

In Cotriade, the Breton fish soup, Muscadet is used in the recipe because it's made in the Loire Valley, which is relatively close to Brittany. Wines from the same or a nearby region are often quite suitable partners for drinking with the soup. This holds true with other spirits as well (see below). However, since no wines are produced in Brittany, you might well serve a very dry cider with this soup. The Bretons often drink it with local fish dishes.

Austrian Grüner Veltliners take well to smooth, fragrant, pale-colored soups. These white wines tend to have nice floral aromas, a full-bodied taste with enough tart acidity to cut through creamy soups and a spicy finish. I love how they accentuate herbs and, in Sautéed Salsify Soup, the white truffle oil used as a final drizzle.

Velouté of Cauliflower, like many creamy preparations, needs a wine with legs and probably some oak, like a wonderful French white Burgundy or well-balanced California Chardonnay. A non-oaky Chardonnay would go with a fish fumet base, as well. Or, you might think of fumé blanc.

For very fresh, light, chilled soups that are yogurt or buttermilk based, from a Dilled Cream of Yellow & Green Squash Soup to Peach Soup with Blueberries, choose a light wine with a bit of spritz or an outright sparkler, like Spanish Cava or even a dry Prosecco.

If you add cubes of foie gras to Creamy Pumpkin Soup with Bacon, a rich Sauternes would be a sensational partnership. For an informing ingredient like lobster, or even crab, that has a hint of sweetness and a rich quality, I'd also choose a sweeter wine, perhaps a nice German Riesling.

For well-spiced soups that are prepared with white wine and include tomatoes, such as Cioppino or Mediterranean Fish Soup, I think the flavors, body, and texture of the soups call for a light red wine. Similarly, some rich chicken-stock-based soups pair nicely with reds, too.

Red wines also make good drinking partners with red soups. Chilled Summer Tomato Soup with Diced Vegetables & Basil Cream is a gazpacho-inspired chilled soup with hints of southern France. Why not try chilled Beaujolais? For Roasted Red Peppers & Paprika Soup, a Spanish Tempranillo or Italian Chianti could be the answer.

But wines aren't the only answer for what to drink with soups. I think sherries are unsung and very versatile as a beverage complementing a wide range of soups. If you have a seafood preparation emphasizing fresher flavors and not a rich, creamy base, go with a Manzanilla or even Fino sherry. Shellfish soup with a roasted quality, like Tomato Bisque with Shrimp, might pair with an Amontillado.

Anything with a caramelized aspect—for example, either Roasted Parsnip Soup with Diced Fennel or Hearty Onion Soup—goes nicely with an Amontillado or Oloroso sherry. As for Pumpkin Black Bean Soup, the final stir of sherry in the soup simply demands that a small glass of the same be served at table. However, most bean soups could use a red wine complement, I think, and a sturdy one.

A little Madeira with oxtail soup is a classic. The fortified wine similarly works magic in Winter Chestnut Soup with Duck Confit and other rich game soups.

Staying off wine for a minute, other beverages I find useful as ingredients for soups include dry French ciders in cheese and fruit-based soups, and sweet cider, particularly with root vegetables. You'll find them as a base in Wild Mushroom Soup with Sage, Dried Apples & Hazelnuts and Sweet Potato, Caramelized Onion & Apple Cider Soup. I serve them as a beverage as well. Sweet cider is also a nice complement to some creamy dessert soups.

For heftier beer/bread soup, think Belgian ales, and with Avocado Guacamole Soup, why not a frosty Mexican beer?

Asian-style soups with a miso or dashi base, or a Mongolian Hot Pot, pair nicely with sake. If there is a strong, smoky shiitake flavor, bring on the Scotch, especially a single malt. (But, just a wee dram, mind you!) Other exotic flavors like lemongrass, Meyer lemon, and kefir lime—with those lovely flowery components—would take well to a Gewürztraminer or a very floral Riesling.

Finally, sparkling wine and Kir are delicious with dessert fruit soups. However, I recently discovered a new option while in Prague: elderflower syrup diluted with ten parts sparkling water. The syrup is available in the United States, and its glorious floral taste reminds me that there are some superb non-alcoholic beverages to serve with soups from savory to sweet.

When going the non-alcoholic route, I might also suggest sparkling and non-sparkling Perry and apple juices—made in England from fermented Perry pears and cider apples (also available in an alcoholic version)—as well as some of the grown-up-style ginger beers now on the market.

# Recipe Index

# Index

164